KICK
ANXIETY

ANNE LAIDLAW

CREATION
HOUSE

Kick Anxiety by Anne Laidlaw
Published by Creation House
A Charisma Media Company
600 Rinehart Road
Lake Mary, Florida 32746
www.charismamedia.com

Unless otherwise noted, all Scripture quotations are from the New King James Version of the Bible. Copyright © 1979, 1980, 1982 by Thomas Nelson, Inc., publishers. Used by permission.

Scripture quotations marked ESV are from the Holy Bible, English Standard Version, copyright © 2001 by Crossway Bibles, a division of Good News Publisher. Used by permission.

Scripture quotations marked TLB are from The Living Bible. Copyright © 1971. Used by permission of Tyndale House Publishers, Inc., Wheaton, IL 60189. All rights reserved.

Scripture quotations marked The Message are from The Message: The Bible in Contemporary English, copyright © 1993, 1994, 1995, 1996, 2000, 2001, 2002. Used by permission of NavPress Publishing Group.

Scripture quotations marked NIV are from the Holy Bible, New International Version. Copyright © 1973, 1978, 1984, 2010, 2011, International Bible Society. Used by permission.

Design Director: Bill Johnson
Cover design by Terry Clifton

Visit the author's website: www.annelaidlawministries.com.

Library of Congress Cataloging-in-Publication Data: 2012943427
International Standard Book Number: 978-1-62136-079-7
E-book International Standard Book Number: 978-1-62136-080-3

12 13 14 15 16 — 9 8 7 6 5 4 3 2

DEDICATION

This book is dedicated to my three children,
Jacob, Rachael and Danielle,
my two in-law children,
Vanessa and Matti,
and my darling granddaughter,
Harriet.

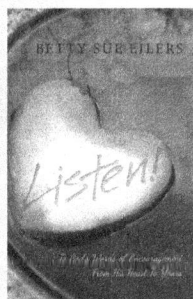

Anne Laidlaw in her books *Know God More*; *Kick Addiction* and in this new book *Kick Anxiety*; has been an inspiration to me both personally and professionally in her relationship with God and in her ability to write and assist others to connect emotionally, mentally and spiritually. In reading and studying her book *Kick Anxiety* she has enabled me to assist clients within my counseling practice who suffer the consequences of inner turmoil and powerlessness; to learn to practice these tools; in connecting their head to their heart; so that they too can come to know the peace God intended; releasing them from the bondage of anxiety to gaining a sense of hope and purpose for a more fulfilling future. Anne has therefore in *Kick Anxiety* capitulated the ability to equip and empower others to ensure God's perfect plan for us all.

—SHARLEEN PARRY
DIP COUNSELING
GRADUATE, CERT ADDICTIVE PROCESSES
COUNSELOR, MEDIATOR, SUPERVISOR

All of us face periods of worry and anxiety as we go through life in a broken and hurting world. In *Kick Anxiety*, Anne Laidlaw tackles the core thoughts and beliefs behind these emotions in a way that draws the reader to face the truth and move closer to their Savior. It is challenging and so readable.

—CHRIS PORTEOUS
BACHELOR OF SCIENCE (BIOLOGY MAJOR),
POSTGRADUATE DIPLOMA OF EDUCATION
(COUNSELING), MASTER OF EDUCATION
(COUNSELING), COUNSELOR, PASTOR

I came about this book at just the right time in my journey with anxiety. *Kick Anxiety* helped me to understand what it was that I was going through, and stepped me through a biblical view of the thoughts and feelings that I had at the time. I truly believe that having this resource enabled me to quickly and thoroughly process things, and therefore allowed me to come out the other side much sooner than I otherwise would have.

—INSTITUTIONAL BANKER, AUCKLAND

ACKNOWLEDGMENTS

I would like to thank my past clients who shared their journeys overcoming anxiety with me. You will not find yourselves in any detail here, but you have added depth and reality to this book.

Also Sharleen Parry for your constant encouragement and belief in the worth of *Kick Anxiety* to facilitate life-changing opportunities for others. And to Chris Porteous and the "Institutional Banker" for your endorsements.

A special thanks goes to Emily Anderson and Eden McCulloch for your help proofreading the text and making suggestions and to Danielle Russel and Rachael Piper for collating and preparing these for my publisher.

My heartfelt thanks goes to my children for their constant encouragement and belief that my work and ministry will continue to impact future generations. And also to Allen Quain, Robert Caggiano, and the team at Creation House for your patience, understanding, professionalism, and excellent preparation to bring this book to print.

And, of course, most of all to our God, our Prince of Peace, who sent His Son Jesus Christ to die on the cross so we are set free to experience His blessed peace in our lives every day.

TABLE OF CONTENTS

FOREWORD

THIS BOOK HAS not been written in a vacuum or void, an oasis of peace nestled in an unreal world. At the time of writing my father has just survived a stroke and numerous seizures that we were called to witness, believing they were his last signs of life on earth. He could not speak for some days but over the following month made a remarkable recovery and is now tired but fully functioning. The company my brother worked for has just closed and he is unemployed. My daughter has just had her twenty-first birthday party with over a hundred guests for which I was chief caterer. Her party was delayed nearly a year because she has been suffering from a severe migraine that has lasted over eighteen months. In the beginning she was in such pain and so drugged I had to bath her like a baby. She is now beginning to improve. My son is preparing for his wedding (this is great news). My ex-husband has sent a lawyer's letter saying he wants to sell the house and expects us out in ten weeks, something I have no intention of doing. And I have just been diagnosed with breast cancer and must undergo surgery, with weeks or months off work including twenty sessions of radiotherapy. This all cuts through the Christmas break so I will have no holiday. God says, "For My thoughts are not your thoughts, Nor are your ways My ways....For as the heavens are higher than the earth, So are My ways higher than your ways, and My thoughts than your thoughts" (Isa. 55:8). And He wasn't kidding. Breast cancer was never on my "to-do" list. It never even seemed a possibility as it does not run in my family. Fortunately God also says, "Many are the afflictions of the righteous, But the LORD delivers him out of them all" (Ps. 34:19). This I am trusting in—for His hand of care can be clearly seen in the proceedings, His touch over-shadowing all the happenings of this time. Let's journey together toward real, inner peace, away from the anxiety and worry of this tumultuous and unpredictable world.

INTRODUCTION

ANXIETY IS A THIEF. It sneaks its way into your heart and steals your energy; your sense of well being; your sense of security; your faith in fellow men, friends, and family; and can even steal your faith in God. It steals your hope in the possibility of a positive future. It drags you toward the negative; toward thoughts of hopelessness, pointlessness, helplessness, inability, failure, and fear. It steals joy, pleasure, and laughter; and it can make you cower, at least on the inside, as you contemplate the problems and reasons not to succeed, the justifications not to even try.

Anxiety isolates. It builds walls to protect you from relationships, even healthy ones, limiting your willingness to share and be all of who you were created to be and to love as you were created to love. It breeds doubt that multiplies, spreading through every area of life, dampening your sense of purpose, and possibly tempting you to manipulate and vainly try to maintain control over circumstances and people around you. It holds you in a state of confusion far from clarity and single-minded vision and drags you into the valley of self-pity.

Anxiety increases adrenaline. It adds hype and tension to every situation, fraying nerves, keeping your body poised in readiness to fight or flee, relentlessly demanding alertness even when you are physically, mentally, and emotionally exhausted. It steals sleep causing you to toss and turn through the night, your mind locked in torturous circles. And left unresolved, anxiety can escalate into panic attacks where your body takes over, seemingly out of control, and embarrasses you, humiliating you in social settings and even alone at home. Or alternatively it can drag you down relentlessly and steadily over time as you sink into a deep pit of depression where you see no escape, where you feel trapped, a victim within your limited vision of reality.

Sometimes your mind may think clearly for a moment and you

briefly glimpse a distant horizon of peace; but your body rarely seems to catch up and instead feels tied to the past by strong merciless emotions, trapped by insidious memories that will not dissolve, that will not release you from their grasp. These memories attempt to prove you are totally incapable of breaking free from this cruel, harsh, unpitying predicament. They are memories that may naggingly remind you that your efforts toward self-release have never worked in the past so how can they possibly work now?

Anxiety seeps into every area of soul and body. It frolics with your mind, repeating thought patterns relentlessly, unforgivingly. It saps your will of its strength to resist and hardens and flicks at your emotions as though playing a game of marbles on a gravel path amidst a turbulent storm. It can penetrate every domain of your body causing stomach upsets, sweats, nervous twitches, and of course those relentless panic attacks. But even deeper than this, anxiety will eventually affect your spirit as you sense a deep inability to cope. Under the strain of merciless feelings of inadequacy, you may gradually feel yourself sinking into that state of despair and inertia that makes you feel distanced, unloved, and ignored in your relationship with God. Where is He when you are feeling this way? Why doesn't He intervene now when you need Him most? Why does He seem to stand back and watch your pain, hiding out of sight?

The sad reality is that anxiety is sin. And, as such, it results in a downward spiral as all cycles of sin eventually do—toward death. It does create distance between you and God and does interfere with your ability to dare to trust Him. But because it is sin, it can be thoroughly dealt with in all its varied symptoms as your spiritual eyes are gradually opened and your focus shifts so that instead of dwelling on yourself and your inabilities, you gradually begin to focus on God and His all-sufficiency, for He is real and He does have a plan for you, even if you cannot see it right now. He also maintains the power to put His sovereign plan into motion if and when He chooses regardless of the will, motives, or plans of anyone else, including you! However He wants to work with you through His grace and your faith to set you free. He may be silent for a time, yet within this silence an amazing opportunity, a gift, is waiting just for you.

This book is a journey aimed at facilitating this change of focus—to assist you open your eyes to see with renewed spiritual clarity and vision, to receive His gift and open the wrappings with purpose and wonder. In the process we will also address some of the unpleasant physical symptoms that accompany this journey so that you may come to experience the reality of a deep and satisfying peace regardless of the circumstances life throws you. For this is where your peace and rest hold their intrinsic value and must be experienced to be real, right where you are now, in the midst of unsavory relationships, ill health, difficult circumstances, and the expansive, mysterious unknown future and whatever surprises it may hold.

Your journey must begin by looking deeply into the reality of your basic, legitimate needs that yearn to be fulfilled, for it is here you begin to become unstuck and follow the anxiety trail. When your deepest desires appear to remain unfulfilled, disappointment and deep hurts can take over and your heart can become sick with deferred hope.

You need to know deep in your heart that this universe is not chaotic in its apparent randomness, that there is a Designer driving historic events. That Someone is in control and He knows what He is doing, even if He doesn't always tell you! And you need to know deep in your heart that this Someone is good.

You need to understand that you have intrinsic value based solely on who you are created to be. You are accepted as you actually are today with all your weaknesses, vulnerabilities, and faults; that your worth is not dependent on how successful, beautiful, intelligent, or athletic you are or how hard you try. Your worth instead relates to that part of you that is deeply known by your Creator, the core essence of your being that is made in His image.

And you need to know there is purpose to your life. Life does hold meaning for you and it matters that you fulfill your potential. You are not just here to live merrily or despairingly and then fall to earth to fertilize the daisies. There is fulfilling work for you to do.

When your basic real needs are not met, you will feel insecure, frightened, and aimless and can become abusive of yourself and others. You are likely to live a life of quiet or frantic desperation, trying to fulfill other people's expectations—or even your own—in a frenzied attempt to promote your self-worth. You may even live a life of avoidance instead of "life" at all as you try to fill the enormous yawning gaps within, using anything you hope will do the trick to fill these holes regardless of how destructive these "things" may be. You may grab at substances, people, material idols, or even philosophical ideas, anything you hope will work. You may become obsessed trying to make it to the "top" in whatever happens to be your personal goal or agenda, trampling others to get there first, or at least to arrive not far from first.

In this fruitless pursuit for meaning and purpose, anxiety often begins to take over as you desperately fear you may not make it. Or worse still, you fear there may be nothing to find when you do get to the place you imagine fulfillment to be. Your search may all be in vain; and at the end of the rainbow after all the struggle and pain, there is merely a mound of dust. Who could stand the disappointment? If this isn't real then what is? Or perhaps you fear that after your long and painful search there will be nothing at all, not even dust! Just space, a huge empty void!

On our journey it is important to remember that some fear is rational. If you venture too close to fire you risk being burnt. Chased by a tornado, it is good to run or hide. Some people are worth avoiding because they are not safe and it is wise to stay away from them. But anxiety does not relate to these rational fears. By its very nature it is irrational. It is based on what could be, might be, or probably should be if certain elements were in place. Yet all of these scenarios are completely beyond your knowledge and out of your control.

Anxiety is based on a play of imagination, exaggeration, and pretense. Researchers claim 95 percent of what you fear will never actually happen! So why waste time worrying and dampen your joy? All the hours spent wading waist deep in anxiety; the sleepless nights; the erratic days, weeks, and even months; are hours, days, and months spent missing out on real life, on the abundant deep meaningful life that is waiting for you.

In our journey toward wholeness and peace, we will seek reality as it actually is; and because of this the journey comes with a warning. Reality as it really exists is unlikely to come on your terms. You may want it to be touchable, tangible, and understandable, clearly labeled on cardboard boxes in alphabetical order. However it rarely, if ever, presents itself this way. Yet in spite of reality's often apparent surprising mysterious emergence, peace will come if you follow this path of reality, and your anxiety will gradually melt away. It will be given permission to be released like a huge sigh that reverberates through your entire being as you finally relax into the arms of an all-powerful, all-knowing Someone who sincerely cares about you and your brief moments on earth. Who is this Someone who can alleviate anxiety, wash your heart with His love, and fill you with His purpose? It is, of course, God Almighty, the Creator of the universe.

Jesus says, "I have come that [you] may have life, and that [you] may have it more abundantly" (John 10:10). Living in fear, in a constant state of anxiety, is not abundant life. You know this in every corner of your being yet you wonder how you can move from worry and incessant anxiety into this place of abundant life. How you can truly leave your fears behind, held in His capable hands? And how you can deal with the knowledge that if you are a believer your companion of anxiety is sin?

Jesus commands you, "Do not worry about your life, what you will eat or what you will drink; nor about your body, what you will put on. Is not life more than food and the body more than clothing?" (Matt. 6:25). Yet how do you actually stop worrying about these basics in life? And what about all the other things that crowd your mind to be anxious about—your health, family, the state of the world? There are endless things to choose to be anxious about.

This word may surprise you. Who would *choose* to be anxious? Yet the truth is—you do choose. We all choose—every day, every moment.

So, where do you begin? Regardless of the causes of your anxiety, there is always one perfect place to start. It is right where you are now! From here you can begin, this moment, by daring to believe that Jesus did in fact come to give you life even if today you don't know what this life looks like. And you can begin to decide to dare to open your heart just a sliver, a tiny crack, to the idea that the almighty Creator of the universe, God, may in fact be able to ensure this abundant, anxiety-free life is truly possible. Are you willing to be open to believe this?

GETTING REAL

Am I anxious?

How long have I been feeling this way?

What physical symptoms do I experience in my anxiety?

Can I identify and label my underlying fears?

Do I believe it is possible to experience deep peace regardless of my circumstances?

If I do, what is stopping me from experiencing this?

Do I believe God can help me?

If you are not a Christian and would like to begin an intimate relationship with your Creator. please pray this simple prayer:

∞

Father in Heaven,

I believe You are the Creator of the universe. I believe You sent Your Son Jesus Christ into this world to die on the cross and rise again after three days to pay the price for my sins, to forgive my sins and set me free. I ask Jesus to come into my heart now. I repent of all the things I have done wrong (name them) and ask You to forgive me. I surrender to You now and ask that You help me live a life to honor You.

In Jesus' name, amen.

*My Name:*_____

Chapter One

WHO'S IN CONTROL?

If only we could believe...

The adequacy of God as our sovereign benefactor, whose way with His servants leaves no ground for any sense or fear of real personal impoverishment at any stage.
—J.I. Packer[1]

Lying on a sandy beach one day on a morning retreat, musing over the concept of abundant life and God's overall sovereignty, I opened my eyes to see gulls flying overhead and marveled at the life in the blue skies. I then noticed the life surrounding me on the sand, tiny insects jumping, hopping, and skipping, hardly visible to the naked eye. And what was happening under the sand where these tiny insects build their homes and others burrow deeply for safety? My eyes then roamed to the seas, the waves crashing against the shore, and I wondered what secrets swam and squirmed, lurking under the water's surface. A whole world of prolific life, all manner of fish, crustaceans, and sea plants yet again invisible to my eye as I gazed at the sun reflecting off the surface. Yet I knew the life was there, living out its destiny. And what about inside my body, the blood pumping, nerves and chemicals transporting detailed information, my heart thumping, everything working with clock-like precision. At least I hoped it was! Such life, and how I depend on it! And deeper still inside, my soul, continually updating me from inside this body of mine; my thoughts, emotions, and will always letting themselves known, frustratingly at times, translating meaning from events, people, and even temperatures that assail me from without. And yet even deeper still there is another order of life, my spiritual

1

life, so alive and encased deep within the belly of this body, a temple, housing the Holy Spirit (God Himself), too wonderful to comprehend. And yet this too, my spiritual life, is not only inside me; it is communicating with God and interacting continually with the outer spiritual sphere, again invisible to my eye. There are angels ministering to God's people bringing refreshment and hope, and there are demons fighting for dominion continually attempting to interfere with and override God's plans. And beyond even this close proximity to human flesh, spiritual life continues out into the heavenlies where these beings, angels and demons, engage in outright warfare. And yet we must still travel beyond again, so far beyond, where God Himself the author and finisher of all life, measures the heavens with the span of His hand (Isa. 40:12).

"In the beginning God created" (Gen. 1:1). Yes, He was there, right at the beginning. He came with power to create life, and He gave us this gift so that now we share in it, me lying on the beach or sitting at my computer, and you engaging with your environment. We possess this gift of life from Him as a function of His grace.

However, He doesn't only create this life and then disappear on holiday. He actively sustains it. "In Him we live and move and have our being" (Acts 17:28). It is His creative power, this same power He used to create the heavens and earth, that now sustains my life and yours every moment, every day, morning and night, even while we are sleeping. "Without Me," God profoundly informs us, "you can do nothing" (John 15:5). And He means it! He is sovereign over the entire universe, over everything in existence. He is ultimately in control over every living and inanimate entity. The Bible clearly makes these astounding claims:

> All the inhabitants of the earth are reputed as nothing;
> He does according to His will in the army of heaven and
> among the inhabitants of the earth. No one can restrain
> His hand or say to Him, "What have You done?"
> —DANIEL 4:35

Yours, O LORD, is the greatness, The power and the glory,
The victory and the majesty; For all that is in heaven and
earth is Yours; Yours is the kingdom, O LORD, and You
are exalted as head over all.
—1 CHRONICLES 29:11

In Your hand is power and might; In Your hand it is to
make great And to give strength to all.
—1 CHRONICLES 29:12

If you feel in any doubt as to the truth of these Scriptures, let's look at a few things God claims sovereignty over. You may be surprised.

God is sovereign in the outpouring of His love, mercy, and grace. Ephesians 1:4–5 states, "He *chose* us *in Him* before the foundation of the world, that we should be holy and without blame before Him *in love*….according to the good pleasure of His will" (emphasis added). We must never forget that "God is love" (1 John 4:8). This is His foremost characteristic and all else flows from this basis including His mercy and grace. He said to Moses, "I will be gracious to whom I will be gracious, and I will have compassion on whom I will have compassion" (Exod. 33:19). In the New Testament in Romans 9:15, Paul repeated this scripture to answer people who were questioning God's way of doing things. They couldn't understand what God was doing or why. Sometimes we don't either, but we must remember that God's basic motivation is always love, which of course includes a desire for what is best for us. How and when He pours out His mercy and grace is determined by His will.

The Bible reveals that God is sovereign over nations and governments. "He has made from one blood every nation of men to dwell on all the face of the earth, and has determined their preappointed times and the boundaries of their dwellings" (Acts 17:26); and this includes the powers within nations. We are told that every authority comes ultimately under God's authority and power (Rom. 13:1).

God even controls how often you need to use your umbrella! He "sends rain on the just and the unjust" (Matt. 5:45). When Elijah prayed God shut the heavens for three years and it did not rain until he prayed again (1 Kings 17:1). In the New Testament Jesus stilled the wind and the waves, taking power away from the storm (Mark 4:39).

Believe it or not, He can control the animal kingdom. He sent ravens to feed Elijah (1 Kings 17:4) and lions to discipline the Assyrians (2 Kings 17:25). He spoke to the prophet Balaam through the mouth of his donkey (Num. 22:28–30). And He feeds all His creatures (Matt. 6:26; Ps. 104:14).

God is sovereign over men's plans. Proverbs 16:9 states "A man's heart plans his way, But the LORD directs his steps." You no doubt will have experienced this in your own life. Even the best laid plans can be mysteriously foiled. Proverbs 21:1 goes even further claiming God's sovereignty over our hearts: "The king's heart is in the hand of the LORD, Like the rivers of water; He turns it wherever He wishes." And yet this in no way takes away your responsibility for your own choices as this is also clearly taught in the Scriptures.

God has sovereignty over good and bad angelic beings. Good angels are called God's "ministering spirits sent forth to minister to those who will inherit salvation" (Heb. 1:14). He commands them and they obey. God defeated the Assyrians using only one angel who killed one hundred and eighty-five thousand men in just one night (2 Kings 19:35). He sent an angel to assure Joseph he should marry Mary, the mother of Jesus, when he discovered she was pregnant (Matt. 1:20). Yet demons must also obey His commands. God sent an evil spirit to trouble King Saul after the king disobeyed Him, turning away to follow his own ideas (1 Sam. 16:14). And when Jesus encountered an evil spirit afflicting a young boy with convulsions, He instantly cast it out (Luke 9:37–42). The spirit had no choice but to obey.

God has control over your reputation, wealth, success, and strength. "Both riches and honor come from You, and You reign over all. In Your hand is power and might; In Your hand it is to make great and to give strength to all....all things come from you" (1 Chron. 29:12, 14). Psalm 75:6–7 reveals God has the necessary power to help whenever you need it! He can make you successful or take your success away. He can give you money or bring you to poverty. He can give you strength and even take this away! "Power belongs to God" (Ps. 62:11).

Your salvation is in God's hands. The apostle Paul declares, "For by grace you have been saved through faith, and that not of yourselves; it is the gift of God, not of works lest anyone should boast" (Eph. 2:8–9). God does not reveal the reason behind His choices, although Ephesians 1:5 assures us they are based on His good pleasure. Because all power belongs to Him you are also assured His choices are not limited by the extent of sin in a person's life unless He chooses to allow it to be. Paul revealed this by saying, "Jesus Christ came into the world to save sinners, of whom I am chief" (1 Tim. 1:15). And look what God did with him. He was a murderer and yet God saved him and gave him the privilege of writing the majority of the New Testament. If He could do this with Paul, He shouldn't have too much trouble with you!

In bringing evidence of God's sovereignty and power, I have used many scriptural references because the Bible claims to contain God's truth: "All Scripture has been given by inspiration of God, and is profitable for doctrine, for reproof, for correction, for instruction in righteousness" (2 Tim. 3:16). If this is true then what is your response to the truths we have explored? If you are like me, you will be speechless at the thorough expanse of God's sovereignty and His absolute ability to control all things and life just as He chooses. And therefore, all we can sincerely do is bow our heads in wonder at our sovereign King and His mighty power and realize that God "is able to do exceedingly abundantly above all that we ask or think, according to the power that works in us" (Eph. 3:20).

However, if He is in control, as He claims to be and the Scriptures reveal, then the question must be asked: Why aren't you allowing Him to take this position in your life?

Anxiety is a way for you to try and control circumstances and people. At a deep level you are believing that worrying will actually make a difference! That it will somehow work and things will go the way you want them to or think they should. Perhaps it is timely, appropriate, and wise to begin to allow God to fill this position and for you to stop trying to keep and maintain control.

If you feel resistant to this idea, where is it coming from? Do you doubt His ability to manage the universe? If so, what do you think He will do that you don't approve of? Be honest with yourself. Perhaps you believe He's responsible for getting you into this mess in the first place! Yet, is this true? Or have you made choices, no matter how unconscious, to help bring yourself to this place? When you stand back for just a moment and look clearly, you may have to admit you have, at least in part.

Now stand back even further and begin to see that although evil has done a great deal of damage in this world, in your life and the lives of people you love, it could have been much worse. Imagine if evil had the full influence for destruction it desires? Something or Someone is restraining evil's power, and surely this is God, for no one else has the necessary power. When you look at the overall state of things, it gradually becomes apparent that perhaps God has managed to do a reasonable job so far, even if you don't like everything He has permitted and done, and even though He may not ask your opinion or permission before He acts or allows someone else to act on their own choices.

You may not understand all that has happened in your life. You may not understand what is happening right now; but you are assured He does and that He has the power to achieve His sovereign will within every circumstance as He chooses. The Bible clearly claims ultimate power belongs to God.

Now let's dig a little deeper. We have already seen that God is sovereign over your salvation, the weather, and all your plans. So what does this mean? If you finally decide to join Him in His will, does this mean He will make you do things against your will? Will you lose your personality? Will you become a doormat to everyone else's whims? These questions are real and important and deserve an answer.

Ultimately, I believe it means God's involvement in your life will cover every aspect of it and He will work in you to will and do His good pleasure (Phil. 2:13). And you are assured this will be for your ultimate good (Rom. 8:28). What a relief! However God likes to work with your cooperation, through you exercising your faith empowered by His grace; so He often stands back and allows you to experience the consequences of your own choices so you can find out what happens when you do things your way. Through this you can learn about your own inability to rule successfully by your own power and it opens your eyes further to your need for Him. He also sometimes allows others to get their way, perhaps causing terrible pain for a time. Through this comes much of the sin done against you by others. And yet, amazingly, through all this apparent evil and chaos, He still promises to bring good for you if you trust Him.

If sovereign power, majesty, and wisdom really do belong to your Lord, the Creator of the universe, and you face this fully, then suddenly your heart will become humbled as you give Him the respect and honor He deserves, for His knowledge and wisdom that so far outreaches your own. He deserves this honor even when you cannot understand the events colliding around you, even when you seem to see sin allowed to prevail in so many situations, and even when you feel afraid. God is not blind. He sees everything going on.

Sit back for a moment, breathe deeply, and contemplate God's greatness as it is revealed in the Scriptures. Remember, the Bible contains God's truth. As you sit and relax, see yourself surrounded by the people you are fearful for, all those you are anxious about. Let them stand before you and slowly dare to take your hands off them one at a time. How does this feel? What could happen? Do you imagine chaos?

Now imagine the King of the universe, your sovereign Lord, placing His loving hands on these people taking over from you where you have left off. How does this feel now? If you are still having trouble giving them into God's care, go back to the Scriptures that describe God's power and sovereignty. Let Him be all of who He is to these people. Sit with this for a while, imagining God's loving hands on each person one by one until you begin to feel more comfortable.

Now comes the hardest part. It is time to do this with yourself. Think of God's sovereign might and imagine placing yourself in the hands of this powerful, loving Creator of the universe, your God. Do you dare do this? What does it feel like? What can happen if He only desires what is ultimately for your good? Remember He says His will is good, acceptable, and perfect (Rom. 12:2). Breathe deeply as you accept this. Now imagine for a moment what it would look and feel like if you left the running of the universe, even your small portion of it, in His powerful capable hands?

Anxiety may begin to grip again as you think of these possibilities. Questions may crowd your mind. What would God do if I let Him take control? If He is in control anyway, then why has He let these terrible things happen? Why does He allow people to sin? Why doesn't He do anything about it, at least the things I think He should do? Allow the questions to push their way into your mind for a moment and then return to the scriptures we have already explored. Now let these scriptures bring calm to your soul. Dwell on these truths. Let them soak into every space in your soul; your mind, will, and emotions. Let them flow over your doubts and dig deeply into the foundations of your spirit, filling every cavern. Dare to believe they are truth. Let them bathe every corner and crevice of your heart. Who is this God who doesn't do things as you would do them? What is He really like? Return to and stay in this chapter until you feel you are making progress here for this is an important part of your foundation and progress.[2]

Once you begin to feel established in these truths, you may discover a problem still remains. No matter how much you read the scriptures we have examined, there is one large question that is unlikely to have been answered. Yes, God may be sovereign and He may be all powerful but does He really care about me personally? Why would He bother? And if He does really care, then wouldn't things be different?

This question must be answered before you will ever feel truly able to dare to trust God in the depths of your soul. We will explore this in the next chapter.

GETTING REAL

Who do I believe is in control overall?

Do I believe God is doing a good job?

Who is in control of my life?

Can I, with my skills, abilities, talents, and personality, do a better job of running the universe than God? Why or why not? Am I being honest about this?

What about my life? In reality can I do a better job running it on my own? Explain.

What thoughts and beliefs do I need to change to make more room for God's sovereignty and power in my life and the lives of my loved ones?

What happens as I dare give those I am anxious about into God's loving hands?

What happens as I dare give myself?

Chapter Two

WHO CARES?

It was a long time before I came to the realization that it is in our acceptance of what is given that God gives Himself.
—ELISABETH ELLIOT[1]

INITIALLY YOU DON'T want to know how important a person is or how much they know. You don't even want to know how powerful they are if you are going to let them into your life or anywhere near your heart. You need to know if they care. Otherwise you are leaving yourself unprotected and making yourself unwisely vulnerable. So how can you receive this knowledge from your all-powerful sovereign God who is so far above you in every way?

God made Himself known to Adam in the Garden after He created him in His own image (Gen. 1:26). He talked and walked with Adam and Eve (Gen. 3:8). He made Himself known to Abraham face to face (Gen. 32:30) and He walked in the midst of the Israelites as they traveled through the wilderness (Deut. 23:14). But God wanted an even more deeply intimate relationship with His people because He saw that they continually went astray the moment He was no longer obviously present. Because of man's sinful disposition inherited from Adam when he sinned in the Garden of Eden and chose independence over God, man cannot maintain his relationship with God in his own power. So God sent His only Son to redeem the situation. He sent Jesus to live a sinless life on earth and then die a cruel, undeserved death to restore man's relationship with Him because of His love for man, because He deeply cared about what was happening to man. We are told, "For God so *loved* the world that He sent

His only begotten Son, that whoever believes in Him should not perish but have everlasting life" (John 3:16, emphasis added).

God's love became action: "When the kindness and the love of God our Savior toward man appeared, not by works of righteousness which we have done, but according to His mercy" (Titus 3:4–5) He sent His Son, Jesus Christ. Jesus walked the earth in perfect obedience to His Father's wishes for thirty-three years, revealing God's love for His people before completing His task. He healed the sick, cast out demons, and set people free, treating them with deep compassion. He taught about God's kingdom to increase their understanding so they could know how to restore their intimate relationship with God. However, the majority of the people did not understand, their eyes being darkened by their sin and unhealthy thinking processes; and so in the end they crucified Him.

But this did not change God's love. In fact it fulfilled it. God works in mysterious ways! Being all-knowing, God knew this would happen and He used the apparent defeat of Christ's death to become the most majestic victory of all time and eternity. Jesus didn't just die and remain dead in the grave. Three days later He rose again in mighty resurrection power. And He still lives, forever, to continue His compassionate care of those who love Him. It is through His painful, torturous death and His subsequent resurrection that God defeated everything that could interfere with your intimate love relationship with Him. This is how much He loves and cares for you.

Total victory has been won with all barriers now removed between you and your Creator, unless of course you choose to put one there. He still allows you to be you. He loves you being you. He created you as you. And of course this means you do have choices. God desires intimacy with *you*. So let's explore this amazing victory in detail.

YOUR SINFUL DISPOSITION

This is the part of you that was inherited from Adam because of his sin. You have no choice in this. Everyone possesses it. It's the part that doesn't need to be taught how to say "No!" It just knows! Ask any two-year-old when they don't get their own way! Yet Christ's death overcame the power of this sinful disposition to control you. Paul reveals this:

> *Therefore [you] were buried with Him through baptism into death, that just as Christ was raised from the dead by the glory of the Father, even so [you] also should walk in newness of life. For if [you] have been united together in the likeness of His death, certainly [you] also shall be in the likeness of His resurrection,* knowing this, *that the old man was crucified with Him, that the body of sin might be done away with, that [you] should no longer be [a slave] to sin. He who has died has been freed from sin.*
> —ROMANS 6:4–7, EMPHASIS ADDED

When Christ died, your sinful disposition, or "old man" as it is also called, died with Him. And notice it says "were." It is in the past tense, so it has already happened. This means that as you believe this truth, sin can no longer have power over you, unless you let it. Believing is the key. We know this because Paul says "knowing this." It is not something you can obey; it is something you need to believe. And as you believe you are set free from the power of sin because of what Christ has done for you, because of God's love. Not only did He conquer this part of you but He also gives you a new life. He says, "If anyone is in Christ, he is a new creation; old things have passed away; behold, all things have become new" (2 Cor. 5:17).

When you are anxious, you are not identifying with or living within this truth. Instead you are allowing sin to have dominion over you. Remember, worry is sin but because of what Christ accomplished on the cross sin can no longer retain power over any part of your life unless you permit it to. Oswald Chambers explains the transfer this way:

> *Redemption means that Jesus Christ can put into any*
> *man the hereditary disposition that was in Himself, and*
> *all the standards He gives are based on that disposition:*
> *His teaching is for the life He puts in. The moral transac-*
> *tion on my part is agreement with God's verdict on sin in*
> *the Cross of Jesus Christ.*[2]

Instead of your sinful disposition ruling your life, now Christ's sinless disposition can rule.

YOUR FLESH

This is your soul, the part that Adam possessed before he sinned in the Garden. It includes your mind, will, and emotions and allows you to make choices that have real consequences. It is also the part that joins with your sinful disposition, is tempted by Satan and worldly influences, and can get into all kinds of mischief. It is the part where worry and anxiety manifest themselves as your mind lingers on unhelpful thoughts and your emotions become entwined in the merry dance these thoughts evoke. With all this activity your will becomes weakened. And, of course, whatever happens in your soul or flesh also affects your body. Thoughts transfer from your mind into your body in a wide variety of anxiety-induced physical reactions. However, through the work Christ accomplished on the cross, through His death and subsequent resurrection, through God's plan of redemption, and by transplanting Christ's own disposition within you, He enables you to master your flesh.

Romans 8:5–6 states, "Those who live according to the flesh set their minds on the things of the flesh, but those who live according to the Spirit, the things of the Spirit. For to be carnally minded is death, but to be spiritually minded is life and peace." It goes on to say that those who live according to the flesh "cannot please God....If you live according to the flesh you will die; but if by the Spirit you put to death the deeds of the body, you will live" (vv. 8, 13). It's pretty clear what needs to happen here! Your flesh must die along with your sinful disposition. It can't just be ignored, stuffed down, made fun of, or indulged in—it must be killed. Paul shows that Christ provided for this when he says:

> *I* have been *crucified with Christ; it is no longer I who live, but Christ lives in me; and the life which I now live in the flesh I live by faith in the Son of God, who loved me and gave Himself for me.*
> —GALATIANS 2:20, EMPHASIS ADDED

Here we see that his unregenerate self has died and Christ has come to live within him, in what he still calls his flesh, but he is now using the word to relate to the workings of his soul—his mind, will, and emotions in their state before sin entered the world through Adam. Notice this has all been accomplished by work only God can do. And God has already completed it. It is only after realizing this in the depths of your being that you are able to live within this truth. This part is your responsibility.

Once this truth is firmly imbedded in your spirit, you need to learn how to live in this new place with your "I" or "self" crucified with Christ. Galatians 5:16 tells you how: "Walk in the Spirit, and you shall not fulfill the lust of the flesh." When talking about the "lust of the flesh," he means following anything that is above seeking to know God and putting Him in the center of your life. So to be able to walk in victory in newness of life in your mind, will, and emotions, you need to learn to "walk in the Spirit."

Before Christ died He told His disciples He would pray to His Father and God "will give you another Helper, that He may abide with you forever—the Spirit of truth; whom the world cannot receive, because it neither sees Him nor knows Him; but you know Him, for He dwells with you and will be in you" (John 14:16–17). This was fulfilled on the day of Pentecost when the disciples were baptized with the Holy Spirit and began to learn to walk in the Spirit. As you learn to listen to the Holy Spirit who dwells within your spirit, and obey His voice, you also will learn to walk in the Spirit.

The Holy Spirit can help you in many ways. He leads you into truth. Through listening to His promptings and receiving revelation through reading your Bible, you can learn how you are to behave in a Christ-honoring manner. You can also be given revelation on what the future may hold. "When He, the Spirit of truth, has come, He will guide you into all truth; for He will not speak on His own authority, but whatever He hears He will speak; and He will tell you things to come" (John 16:13). He can help your understanding enabling you to keep things in perspective by reminding you of what God has done in the past (John 14:26). He can teach you about God's kingdom and His ways and the purposes and plans He has for you (John 14:26; 16:13). He gives you spiritual gifts to enable you to obey and succeed in your work (Acts 2:4; 1 Cor. 12). He can direct your ministry (Acts 16:6), prepare you for service (Rom. 7:6) and reveal God's love to you filling you with hope (Rom. 5:5). He gives you power to tell others about Jesus (Acts 4:33). And He blesses you with a sound mind to understand His ways and purposes and gives you the power you need to overcome fear and anxiety, with the knowledge that His endless and generous love will strengthen you (2 Tim. 1:7).

Anxiety manifests itself in your flesh. This is where you feel it and also where you need to overcome much of it. It plays with your mind, weakens your will, and sabotages your emotions. It is only the power of the Holy Spirit working within you that will enable you to overcome your anxiety as you learn to "walk in the Spirit," bringing your mind, will, and emotions in line with God's mind and His will for your life. In the process your emotions will be restored.

OVERCOMING SATAN

Besides the impulses of the flesh, Satan is your fiercest foe. He was a liar in the beginning and still is. Your flesh, influenced by your sinful disposition, is vulnerable, weak, and can be easily influenced by Satan. He knows this only too well. He revels in it and roams around like a roaring lion to see whom he may devour. He especially targets fleshly Christians, assaulting them, tempting their minds by presenting negative and unhealthy thoughts. When successful here, emotions soon become involved; and once he gains a foothold in this area, it is not long before the person's will bends and soon wants to follow Satan's suggestions. Your body just goes along for the ride doing whatever your mind thinks of next. Satan knows exactly how to take advantage of your weak spots and play with them. He has had centuries of practice. But thankfully, Christ knows every one of Satan's tricks. He is not fooled for a moment. What is more, He conquered Satan once and for all when He died on the cross and rose in resurrection power overcoming the final obstacle—death.

> *Christ having disarmed principalities and powers, He made a public spectacle of them, triumphing over them.*
> —COLOSSIANS 2:15

This victory ensures that "He [Christ] who is in you is greater than he that is in the world" (1 John 4:4); and He always will be. Remember, all power belongs to God.

However, through God's love for you, Christ's victory means even more in your defense against Satan; because through His perfect obedience He not only defeated death but was also given all authority for life. In Matthew 28:18 He says, "All authority has been given to Me in heaven and on earth." In this authority, given to Him by His Father, Jesus then gives each of His disciples authority over Satan and all demons. We see this in Luke 9:1 where He called them together and "gave them power and authority over all demons, and to cure diseases." If you are one of His disciples, you also have this authority and power in Christ.

Satan can have no power over you unless you let him. He can try and tempt you, but even here God promises you will not be tempted beyond your ability to cope. "No temptation has overtaken you except such as is common to man; but God is faithful, who will not allow you to be tempted beyond what you are able, but with the temptation will also make the way of escape, that you may be able to bear it" (1 Cor. 10:13). You have also been given spiritual armor to wear to protect you and once donned all you need to do is stand to receive your victory (Eph. 6:11–18).

To maintain success you must learn to live in the authority you have been given, wearing your armor at all times. You can bind Satan's power in prayer using your authority in Christ's name as a member of God's family. When you pray in Jesus' name knowing Him as Lord of your life, Satan has no choice but to obey.

WORLDLY INFLUENCE

The world comprises of the "lust of the flesh, the lust of the eyes, and the pride of life" (1 John 2:16). It is all the stuff you want because it looks good or someone else has it or it feels good, but it may not be good for you and it may not be part of God's plan for your life. It is the world that Satan uses in his attempts to entice you away from God's best. The world is one of Satan's tools in the toy box of his temptations. However, here again you find Christ has overcome the power of these influences that try to take your flesh captive and bring you into bondage.

> For whatever is born of God overcomes the world. And this is the victory that has overcome the world—[your] faith.
> —1 JOHN 5:4

Who is your faith in? It is in Christ and the work He has accomplished on the cross, of course, and not in yourself. From this place in Christ, your temptations will grow strangely dim and lose their power over you.

God loves you so much. He cares so much about you that He gives you these permanent eternal victories to give you freedom. It has all been accomplished through the work Jesus Christ did on the cross. Through His victory:

- Your sinful disposition is dead in Christ,

- Your flesh has been crucified,

- Satan has been disarmed and has no authority over you,

- You have victory over the world.

These four areas include everything that attempts to stop you from living in obedience to Christ; and it is because God loves you so deeply and cares about you so sincerely, that He has given you these victories. Now it is up to you to learn to live in them. "But thanks be to God, who gives us the victory through our Lord Jesus Christ" (1 Cor. 15:57).

However, God's love in its amazing expanse extends so much further than even these astounding victories because He also commands His supernatural angels to take care of you (Heb. 1:14). He gives His Holy Spirit to live within to guide you and He showers you with spiritual gifts (1 Cor. 12:1–11, 28). He brings human support by directing you to bear other's burdens as they bear yours (Gal. 6:2), and to pray for each other (James 5:16). He teaches humility by commanding us to submit to each other (Eph. 5:21), serve one another (Gal. 5:13), be kind to one another (Eph. 4:32), teach one another (Col. 3:16), exhort one another (Heb. 3:13; 10:25), and love one another (Rom. 13:8; 1 Thess. 3:12; 1 John 3:11). You are never alone!

And where does this bountiful love leave you? What does it give you? Through receiving it you are now free to change, free to enter into the resurrection abundant life Christ died to give you, to live within the peace and rest that Christ's victory brings, regardless of the circumstances surrounding you.

GETTING REAL

Do I believe God cares for and loves me?

What evidence do I have that He does?

In what four areas has Christ's death on the cross won victory for me?

What has this achieved for me?

Am I "walking in the Spirit" or in the flesh?

How can I change?

Am I willing to learn to change?

Chapter Three

WHAT IF?

As a father pities his children, So the LORD
pities those who fear Him, For He knows our
frame; He remembers that we are dust.

—PSALM 103:13–14

WHAT IF GOD goes on holiday and forgets you're waiting to
be picked up at the bus stop? What if your spouse deserts you
or your child dies in a car accident? What if you get cancer?
What if the share market collapses or your business goes bankrupt? What if a tsunami sweeps away everything you own or war
breaks out tomorrow? What if your best friend is murdered or
you are raped? What if you discover your parents never loved
you?

Most anxiety camps around things that "could" happen or
that you could find out rather than things that have actually
happened or are true. You are very good at imagining the worst
possibilities—and why not? Terrible things have happened in
the past—occasionally—and you remember them well. And
this can be where part of your problem lies because good things
have also happened in the past—so why don't you remember
them first?

King David fell into this dilemma and he cried out, "You hold
my eyelids open; I am so troubled that I cannot speak....Will
the Lord cast off forever? And will He be favorable no more?
Has His mercy ceased forever? Has His promise failed forever-
more? Has God forgotten to be gracious?" (Ps. 77:4, 7–9). David
was so distraught he couldn't sleep. He couldn't see a solution
to his problem. He wondered if God had forgotten him. He

knew everything was somehow in God's hands but God wasn't speaking!

And sometimes God is silent. Sometimes you are left not knowing what is happening. Not knowing where to turn. Not having a clue what to do. Not even knowing what is true. What is around the corner? Is a train coming full speed toward you on tracks with no space to jump clear or is a parade to celebrate your success going to appear? And you dread finding out. Why? Because maybe you won't be able to cope! Maybe you will be overwhelmed! Maybe you will be bankrupt! Maybe your loved one will leave! Maybe they will die! Maybe you will die! What if any of this happens? And why isn't God showing up? Where is your comfort? Where is your help?

Even success has its questions. Where will it lead? Will you cope with the added pressure? Will you become arrogant? Will you lose your friends and gain a bunch of fake ones? Will you get paid more? Can you maintain your righteousness and still be successful? Success can be a test just as full of temptations as all the difficult circumstances that can overwhelm your life.

Anxiety breeds and multiplies among these "what ifs" as your imagination meanders into fantasies. As Stanley Jones once wrote, "Worry is the advance interest you pay on troubles that never come."[1] The possibilities, swamped with chemical stimulants, travel from your mind into your stomach producing acid which disrupts your whole bodily system stealing rest and sleep. And it can be relentless. This happened to me recently over a passing comment a friend made. He didn't have time to elaborate. But I did! In technicolor, for hours through the darkness! I'm sure I imagined scenarios he had never dreamed of. Two days later when I caught up with him again and heard the whole story, none of my imaginings had been correct. So what can we do?

As King David lay tossing upon his bed, he decided to change his thinking. And it was hard work. He had to tell himself firmly: "I will remember the years of the right hand of the Most High. I will remember the works of the LORD; Surely I will remember

Your wonders of old. I will meditate on all Your work, and talk of Your deeds" (Ps. 77:10–12). And using His will, he began to reflect on the attributes of God as a way to bring his life back into perspective. "Your way, O God, is in the sanctuary; Who is so great a God as our God? You are the God who does wonders; You have decided Your strength among the peoples, You have with Your arm redeemed Your people" (vv. 13–15). He encouraged himself in the Lord. And this is something you can do too.

Depending on your disposition and thinking habits, the future can hold either intense fear or opportunity. However, your disposition does not need to rule your life. Remember, Jesus died on the cross so you can change those parts of you that are not helpful. You are not stuck with your sinful disposition in charge, you can receive the disposition of Christ and learn to walk with God "in the Spirit" being led by Him on a daily basis.

When God called Abraham to leave his home, work, and family and set out on the road to a strange land, Abraham went "not knowing where he was going" (Heb. 11:8). One day God may call you to do a similar thing. You may never need to leave your house, of course, but you may be called to follow Christ in a new way, to start a new activity. You may feel the strong pull of His calling, even see a vision of the end result, but have no idea how you are going to get there. It is in these times you need to remember your walk with God is a walk of faith. He promised Jeremiah, "I know the thoughts I think toward you, says the LORD, thoughts of peace and not of evil, to give you a future and a hope" (Jer. 29:11). This promise is for you also.

Notice God says His thoughts and therefore His plans are for your peace. He does not want you to walk in turmoil and confusion but instead in faith and peace, believing He has made the way straight even if you can't see very far ahead at the moment, even if you are walking through a war zone. He says His word is a lamp to your feet and a light to your path (Ps. 119:105). He never guarantees a spot lit arena—only a path, and sometimes this path may seem very narrow, dim, and misty. Jesus, in His kindness, warns of this. He says, "Narrow is the gate and difficult is the way which leads to life, and there are few who find it" (Matt. 7:14). However, there will always be enough light to take the next step. The trick is to stay on the path, if you are going in the right direction, even if you can only see one small footstep at a time. Of course if you discover you are going in the wrong direction, you will need to repent, turn 180 degrees around, and go back to the point where you left the narrow path and then continue on from there, even if this means making some very difficult decisions. For your life to be full of God's peace and rest instead of fear and anxiety, you must walk on the path He has chosen for you.

However, God is not only interested in the distant future and your next small footprint, He is also interested in everything you do along the way and He has carefully planned your progress. Paul assures you, "[You] are His workmanship, created in Christ Jesus for good works, which God prepared beforehand that [you] should walk in them" (Eph. 2:10). Your job is to ask God to tell you clearly the next thing He wants you to do, and then once you know, to obey by faith leaving the consequences up to Him. This walk of faith is not blindly living in false security; it is trusting in God's character and His ability to take care of the details.

You must face the reality that sometimes God will lead you into difficult circumstances. I'm sure Daniel didn't relish being in the den with lions and Stephen didn't choose to be stoned to death. Jesus wasn't too happy about being nailed to the cross either. He sweat blood wrestling with His obedience (Luke 22:44). However, each did walk their next step by faith, trusting God to show them the way and be with them in whatever happened.

Usually you will never know the outcome of your obedience before you obey. This is not your problem. As Elisabeth Elliot reveals in her book *On Asking God Why*, "The disciple cannot test the answer in terms of earthly success or satisfaction or solutions."[2] You must come to a place of trusting the wisdom of your heavenly Father, believing He has your best interests at heart, regardless of what you see with your eyes.

You may be wondering how you can ever get to this place of quiet trust regardless of the turmoil you are facing now or could face in the future, and we will come to this. However, before we journey on to this discovery, we will pause during the next chapter to find different ways to deal with the bodily symptoms often attached to anxiety. Why carry their burden any further when you don't need to?

<u>GETTING REAL</u>

How much time do I spend worrying about things that have not yet happened?

Do I lose sleep worrying about them?

Does my worrying and anxiety help solve my problems?

What else could I do?

How is my faith walk?

What is my faith based on?

Chapter Four

SORTING STUFF

Anxiety in the heart of a man causes depression.
—PROVERBS 12:25

BEING PREOCCUPIED WITH anxious thoughts is a little like nibbling an appetizer from the fiery depths of hell. It brings a portion of death with each bite that permeates and disrupts every part of life including sleeping, dreaming, eating, and relating to others. It steals time and energy and drains life's zeal, snuffing it out before it even sparks. Anxiety seems to magnify all negative responses from restlessness, self-absorption, unreasonable self-blame, and criticism to exhaustion, lack of concentration, over-eating, and compulsive behaviors. And it minimizes anything that even whiffs of wholesomeness. You tend to revert to the powerlessness and hopelessness sometimes experienced in childhood and become a victim to your meandering thoughts and exaggerated physical sensations. Let's sort a few basics. The temptation may be to skip this chapter but resist. This is essential to your wellbeing.

BREATHING

One of first things to happen when you are anxious is that you stop breathing properly. Your breathing becomes short, shallow, and centered in your chest. Correct breathing is essential to balance body chemistry, and it is very easy to adjust. Right where you are sitting put your hand on your stomach and taking in a deep breath through your nose make sure your hand rises up as this breath fills the base of your lungs. Then release the air through your mouth. Continue to do this for five deep breaths. Notice the change in your body chemistry. The results are instant. Calmness will begin spreading throughout your body. Now, every time you feel anxious start with this breathing exercise to release your body from tension. From this place you will be able to think more clearly.

Relaxation

When you are anxious your body loses its ability to relax. After remedying your breathing, the next step is to do a simple relaxation exercise that can be completed wherever you are whether driving, watching television, or working at a desk. It will sharply reduce your anxiety level and no one will suspect a thing!

Start with your toes. Squeeze the muscles tightly then slowly release. Next squeeze your calves—and slowly release. Then your thighs and buttocks—squeeze and slowly release. Do the same to your stomach area, then your chest. Next squeeze your arms and upper back. Then, try your neck. You may look a little strange as you do this one! Finish off with a deep breath with your hand on your stomach and feel your stomach rise up (rather than your shoulders) and then relax. Experience the release in your body. This exercise works! If there is still tightness in any area of your body return to this place and repeat. Feel the blood flow. Repeat whenever necessary.

Food

Few people like making changes to their diet. We are creatures of habit and often indulgence. And the problem with dietary changes, as with many adjustments, is that it takes a little while to see positive results. But let's start by being honest. Are you overweight? Are you underweight? Do you indulge in frequent junk food? Is most of your food natural or processed?

It is now well-known and well-advertised that the more natural and, therefore, raw your food is, the better it is for you. It is also well-researched that additives, colorings, preservatives, and an excess of sugar can create health problems and mood swings. Therefore, if you are suffering from anxiety, it is wise to eliminate these items from your diet as much as possible. Read food labels in the supermarket. Choose natural ingredients. Learn how to cook simple nutritious meals. Learn to love raw food. Make salads interesting by adding seeds, fresh herbs, nuts, and sprouts. Even children can be taught to love salads. It will only take a few weeks, and you will notice the difference. Your head will feel clearer, you will be more alert, your moods will be steadier, and your life will feel more manageable.

BEVERAGES

What do you drink regularly—coffee, tea, sweetened fizzy drink, alcohol? Too much of any of these beverages will make you feel anxious regardless of anything else going on in your life. Even too much milk can put on weight and make you feel gluggy—if there is such a word! Obviously the best beverage choice is fresh water. This is closely followed by herbal teas. Many varieties are now available. You can grow a few herbs in your garden or in pots on your windowsill. Find a flavor you like. And remember it can take time to begin to enjoy any new taste. Try one for a month; you may be surprised.

EXERCISE

Taking regular daily exercise is a well-researched stress reliever. It does not matter whether you walk, run, go to the gym, skip, swim, or jump on a trampoline—your whole body inside and out as well as your mind will benefit. You will feel fresher, be more clear-headed and sleep better. If you are not already exercising regularly, start today. Begin with an amount of exercise realistic for you, and then slowly build your time up to at least four half-hour sessions a week. It won't be long before you wouldn't miss them for anything. You can also choose to make new healthy choices each week. Walk up stairs instead of taking the elevator. Walk to the shops instead of driving your car. Meet a friend for a walk in the park instead of coffee and cake in a café. Be creative.

SLEEP

Maintaining regular sleep patterns and an appropriate amount of sleep is essential for a healthy mind and body. Most people benefit best from between seven to eight hours sleep a night, but this will vary with age and health. Develop a relaxing routine before going to bed if you have trouble dropping off to sleep. Perhaps take a warm bath and read a book for a short time. Then turn out your light and move into your favorite sleeping position.

If anxious thoughts threaten to keep you awake, realize that your mind may be playing with these thoughts now because you didn't take time to think them through adequately before you went to bed. Keep a note pad and pen beside your bed and write down the issues, telling yourself you will think about them tomorrow. Remind yourself that now is the time to sleep, not think. Then return to your favorite sleeping position and breathe deeply. If you still have trouble dropping off to sleep, try repeating your favorite restful scripture verse over and over again in your mind. Then next day take time to think through important issues.

If your problem is waking in the middle of the night, go to the bathroom, then keeping warm, go to a quiet room and read something very boring for about ten minutes under a dim light. Return to bed and your favorite sleeping position, take a few deep breaths to relax your body and repeat as before. If you still have trouble, a small glass of milk may help by altering your stomach chemistry producing a more alkaline environment. If the problem remains, try a variety of healthy alternatives such as reading a psalm, herbal remedy, or imagining your favorite holiday; and if all fails and the problem persists, seek professional help.

SAFETY

Everyone needs a safe place of retreat, especially when life seems overwhelming. And sometimes a safe place is hard to find right where you are today. However, it is possible to create one that is available anytime you need it regardless of your environment.

Real safety is only found in God's presence, encased in the

wonder of all of who He is. You may have experienced this wonderful sense of peace at times in the past. Close your eyes and remember a time or place when you have experienced your greatest safety, warmth, and love. It may relate to a time or place in your childhood, a past holiday, or a time spent in the quietness of communion with God. Now imagine this space, keeping your eyes closed, and be there in all its detail. Feel the feelings associated with this space. Let them flow. Can you feel the feelings? Keep yourself there until you do. Once you can feel these warm comforting feelings, "anchor" them to your body. You do this by choosing a physical movement that can be repeated unobtrusively wherever you may be, such as pressing your thumb and forefinger together at the tip or pressing the side of your wrist with the opposite hand's thumb. As you press, this will "anchor" the good feelings associated with your "safe place" with this physical action. This is your "anchor point." Press hard as you continue to feel the safe feelings. Then stop and relax. Do this three times so the association is firmly established. This simple but effective process actually connects the "safe place" and "anchor point" within your brain. It makes a new pathway that you can return to at will.

To check that you have established your "anchor point" effectively, close your eyes again and this time think of a terrible time in your life. Feel the feelings associated with this terrible experience. Once you are immersed in these bad feelings, shout "Stop!" to yourself out loud (you only need do this the first time) and then in your mind quickly go to your "safe place." Press hard on your "anchor point" with the physical action you choose and close your eyes, returning to your "safe place" with all the wonderful feelings again. Notice how quickly this change in mental association changes your actual feelings. Practice this process a number of times to ensure you are able to go to your "safe place" quickly and effectively.[1]

As you go about your normal life, next time you feel anxious, press your "anchor point" and go to your "safe place." This will stop your anxious feelings quickly and allow you to escape from the tyranny of these feelings; and it will give you time, space, and energy to move on to the next stage of dealing with the underlying issues causing your anxiety.

GETTING REAL

Is my breathing normally shallow, centered in my chest, or deep and felt within my stomach? If I am breathing with shallow breaths how can I change this?

Am I willing to use relaxation exercises regularly to help relieve bodily tension?

What are my eating habits? Will I change to more raw and fresh food? How can I do this practically?

What do I usually drink? If necessary am I willing to change my habits in this area?

Have I found my "safe place" and "anchor point"? Am I willing to practice this on a regular basis until I can go to my "safe place" quickly?

Does it work?

Chapter Five

REALITY

*Christianity got over the difficulty of com-
bining furious opposites, by keeping them
both, and keeping them both furious.*
—G.K Chesterton[1]

REALITY CAN HURT. And no one welcomes pain. Sometimes
you may not want to know the truth about yourself and the way
you react to different situations because you don't live up to your
own expectations, or anyone else's. No one likes to fail according
to their own measure of success or the measure held by those
they love. Yet in order to come into a new phase of abundant
life, quiet trust, and peace, you will need to face the stark truth
about yourself and the way you relate to others. And you will
need to deal with this truth in a healthy manner even though it
may cause pain, even though your flesh may scream wanting to
divert your attention onto something else, anything to avoid the
actual issues.

This is where anxiety, addictions, and compulsions play their
major role. They are used in a wayward attempt to avoid emotional pain and maintain control over your environment on
your terms. They always lead to bondage and death, even though
in the beginning they may seem innocent and appear to give
satisfaction. Think of a partygoer who begins using alcohol to
feel more sociable and less anxious about meeting new people
and then gradually over time extends this into drinking every
day, even during the day. Or a drug addict who experiences his
first fix and briefly goes to a place of euphoria. However, this
intense feeling will never be as good again, even though he will

use different or higher doses of drugs in a fruitless attempt to achieve it. No substitutes to finding real abundant life ever truly enhance life but instead always lead to greater and deeper problems and darkness and take you further away from God and His plans for you. However, doing things God's way always leads to greater light, even though the path may seem clouded and difficult along the way at times.

You may think it strange to consider you use anxiety to avoid truth in your life. It is no stranger than using drugs, alcohol, relationships, television, ministry, work, sex, or all the other things people use to try and get their needs met *their* way. Through a distorted way of thinking, the pain that can be associated with these diversions and distractions somehow seems less painful than the pain attached to dealing with the actual issues that are at the core of the real problem.

I call this thinking "distorted" because the basic assumption is not true. Somehow you are thinking that if you do "this" (i.e., be anxious) then your problem will be solved. If you don't worry about it, who will? And surely worry is the "best" way to solve problems! Yet sadly, as you have discovered, this method leads deeper into bondage. God's Word says, "For my people have done two evils; they have forsaken Me, the Fountain of Life-giving Water; and they have built for themselves broken cisterns that can't hold water!" (Jer. 2:13, TLB). Anxiety is a broken cistern. It cannot produce the results you are seeking. As you have already discovered it cannot give you the peace and rest you long for and what's more it does not solve anything.

The core problem usually relates to a real need or needs that are not being met. And because you don't know how to meet these needs you cover them with lesser "quick fixes," even though these "lesser" issues become major life-limiting bondages. All symptoms such as alcoholism, anorexia, anxiety, and most forms of depression develop in this way. If you suffer from any of these and many other forms of malfunctioning behavior you are attempting to cover up the real issue and are using your unhealthy behavior to avoid reality. Sadly, your cover-up inevitably becomes your cage, and you are soon trapped in a self-destructive cycle that can spiral more and more out of control until you decide to do things differently. If you keep doing the same thing, you will keep getting the same result.

Your unmet needs relate to the three basic needs we looked at in the first three chapters. "Who is in control?"—your security; "Who cares?"—your self-worth and desire for love; and "What if?"—your significance and purpose. Once these three needs are met, and as we have seen they can only be met in a real relationship with God, then you are on the road to recovery. To the extent you attempt to meet these needs anywhere else, you will find disappointment and hurt. Of course, I am not suggesting you don't enjoy the additional bonuses friends, family, careers, finances, and fun can add to these needs being satisfied; but the problem with relying on these blessings is that they can unexpectedly disappear. Your friends may dump you, your spouse may leave, you may lose your job, or the stock market may collapse. Whereas, God alone is always available, always present, and eternally powerful. He promises, "I will never leave you nor forsake you" (Heb. 13:5). And because He is the only Being unlimited by time, knowledge, wisdom, or power, He is the only One who can truly keep His promise.

If you wish to have your basic needs of security, self-worth, and significance met in Christ, you need to be in an intimate relationship with Him. If you have not already made this decision and would like to, perhaps it is time to pray the simple prayer at the end of the Introduction (page xix).

Now, firmly established in a relationship with God, you must face the fact that sin is the cause of much of your anxiety. King David cried out, "There is no soundness in my flesh Because of Your anger, Nor any health in my bones Because of my sin....I am feeble and severely broken; I groan because of the turmoil of my heart" (Ps. 38:3, 8). The only solution to sin is to come in genuine repentance before God and ask for forgiveness. If you do this in sincerity of heart with your whole being God promises, "If

[you] confess [your] sins, He is faithful and just to forgive [your] sins and cleanse [you] from all unrighteousness" (1 John 1:9).

There is no shortcut to the peace found through forgiveness, although you may have attempted to find one. God is very clear about this. When Jesus started His ministry, His primary message was "repent, for the kingdom of God is at hand" (Matt. 3:2). Repentance is fundamental in any relationship with God. It is not negotiable. Genuine repentance always precedes forgiveness and the resulting freedom that flows from it. Remember, anxiety itself is sin, so you will need to include this in your repentance; but there will also be many other wrong decisions that have led to your anxiety. These all need to be faced in the depths of their reality and repented of so you are cleansed and free to begin your new life of trust and peace. If you have not already entered into the reality and rewards of repentance and would like to, pray this simple prayer:

> *Father in Heaven,*
> *I understand I have sinned against You. I repent of (name the areas and issues) and ask You to forgive me.*
>
> *Thank You, in Jesus' name, Amen.*

If your heart is sincere, God assures you that you are forgiven (1 John 1:9). However sin is not the only culprit that can cause anxiety. Sometimes unfortunate life circumstances may have brought you to this place of anxiety and your faith is being sorely tested. If this is so, Peter assures you, "Beloved, do not think it strange concerning the fiery trial which is to try you, as though some strange thing happened to you" (1 Pet. 4:12). Life can deal many unsavory experiences over which you have no control, and they can be extremely painful. This is where the "furious opposites" in the quote at the beginning of this chapter become apparent and are held fiercely in tandem in your walk with God. On the one hand He promises to bless you, while on the other hand Jesus promises, "In the world you will have tribulation" (John 16:33). The Christian's journey is not an easy one! You will suffer along the way. Yet Jesus finishes this statement with the revelation of how these two furious and annoying opposites actually fit together. He says, "But be of good cheer, I have overcome the world." As we have seen, Christ overcame the destructive power the world can have over you when He died on the cross and rose in resurrection power. He has won the victory for you. Now you need to learn how to enter into this victory to experience peace in every circumstance.

The apostle Peter's continuing words may help you view suffering in a more positive perspective as you dare to face your own reality. After acknowledging the possibility and presence of fiery trials, he says, "But rejoice to the extent that you partake of Christ's sufferings, that when His glory is revealed, you may be glad with exceeding joy. If you are reproached for the name of Christ, blessed are you, for the Spirit of glory and of God rests upon you" (1 Pet. 4:13–14). Nothing is hidden from Jesus' sight. He has even counted the hairs on your head! He knows what you have been through and are going through. He suffered also, and He was innocent. Christ's suffering was so intense He sweated blood. In His flesh He didn't want to hang on a cross, yet He obeyed God's plan for His life from His heart. Through His painful experiences, "He learned obedience by the things which He suffered" (Heb. 5:8) because He did not turn away from God in the midst of His trials.

If He needed to experience suffering to learn obedience, you are no different. Yet even Jesus needed an incentive to help Him persevere through His trials successfully. And He shares His secret. It was "the joy that was set before Him" that enabled Him to keep going (Heb. 12:2).

Whatever has caused your suffering, whether it is your sin, the sin of others, or adverse circumstances, God wants you to face the reality of where you are right now and understand how you arrived at this place. King David says of God, "You desire truth in the inward parts, and in the hidden part You will make me to know wisdom" (Ps. 51:6). God will help you if you ask Him. He has given you the Holy Spirit for this purpose (John 16:13).

Ask God to reveal truth to you, and humbly come before Him in repentance where you need to. Everyone falls short of God's perfect holiness, so you are not alone. Be honest with yourself.

Facing reality does not only mean facing the reality in your own life as you live day to day, it also means facing the reality of other people's lives and how they have impacted you. The purpose of this is not to place blame on others and absolve yourself from responsibility. Instead it requires an honest look at the facts, an appraisal of where responsibilities lie in different circumstances; and then it requires an acceptance of your own responsibility for your responses, even to other people's sin, and an acceptance of other people's responsibility. This acceptance does not necessarily mean agreement.

You are always responsible for your own actions and reactions, regardless of other people's involvement. As an adult no one can make you do anything unless you let them (except where physical force is used). You are also responsible for your emotional responses. You allow yourself to feel angry, sad, or happy. At times, of course, all these feelings are appropriate. However, if anger or grief is left unresolved, they can overtake your life in unhealthy proportions and you may need the help of a counselor to assist you resolve the underlying issues.

Identifying your responsibility also highlights other people's responsibility. Yet they may also be trying to avoid owning their own responsibility, and this can in turn further impact your life. If they are not taking responsibility, you may need to consider various options. Firstly, you may decide to confront them in love, revealing their problem and responsibility with the view of offering them the opportunity to repent. If they will not listen, I advise you take Christian witnesses with you to confront them again. If they still refuse to acknowledge their harmful behavior, the matter should be brought before the Church if they are Christians. You may also need to distance yourself from such people until they decide to change or contact police and follow legal proceedings if this is appropriate.

Facing reality also means facing the reality of who God is.

Your God is an awe-inspiring God. His character is perfect, His ways are perfect, His knowledge is perfect, His love is faultless. Everything about Him embodies absolute perfection. The more you come to know Him in His vastness, the stronger your faith and foundation will become. Christ is the Rock (1 Cor. 10:4). He is your Rock, the only faultless, firm foundation you can utterly rely upon. The best way to get to know God more is to read your Bible and find out more about Him. Read books that tell you about Him. Study His personal characteristics, His graciousness, His love, His goodness, His severity, His holiness. My own book *Know God More* takes forty-four of God's characteristics and discusses them in detail using scriptural references to help build faith as you discover the wonders of who He is. Spend quality time in prayer with Him, speaking and listening to His Spirit speak within your heart. Prayer is your spiritual hotline to eternity. As you come to know God more, your faith will increase; and as your faith grows, your trust will also begin to expand into new areas. In the next chapter we will explore seven interferences that can meddle in this journey.

Getting Real

What realities have I been avoiding regarding my behavior, thoughts, desires, and feelings?

What is the truth?

In what areas do I need to repent?

Have I come in humble repentance and prayed for forgiveness?

Am I forgiven?

Am I allowing God to meet my basic needs of security, self-worth, and significance?

What realities about other people's lives have I been avoiding facing?

What are their God given responsibilities?

Are they facing up to these?

What can I do about this?

How can I begin to know God more so my faith will grow?

Chapter Six

LITTLE FOXES

*Some people assume worry is the result of too much
thinking. Actually it's the result of too little thinking in the
right direction. If you know who God is and understand his
purposes, promises and plans, it will help you not to worry.*
—JOHN MACARTHUR[1]

BEING FIRMLY ESTABLISHED in relationship with God through
genuine repentance, feeling cleansed and forgiven, and beginning to implement changes in your physical symptoms and environment, it is now time to move deeper into the realm of your
mind. It is "the little foxes that spoil the vines" (Song of Sol. 2:15).
The trouble with little foxes is that they grow up to become big
foxes! Foxes are quick, crafty, and surprisingly powerful, and so
are your thought processes. We will look at four major areas that
can profoundly affect your level of anxiety—doubt, unbelief, self-
pity, and double-mindedness—and then briefly site three others.
As you tame these foxes, your anxiety will begin to dissolve and
fruitful vines will flourish.

DOUBT

Doubt cuts off revelation. It prevents you from receiving wisdom
and insight from God.

> *If any of you lacks wisdom, let him ask of God, who gives
> to all liberally and without reproach, and it will be given
> to him. But let him ask in faith, with no doubting, for he
> who doubts is like a wave of the sea driven and tossed*

by the wind. For let not that man suppose that he will
receive anything from the Lord.
—JAMES 1:5–7

If you are constantly doubting God's Word and His character, you are not basing your life on the solid foundation of who He is. This is why a life of doubt is likened to a wave in the sea—there is nothing to hold it in shape; it is all over the place, moving and changing continually with the wind and pull of the tides.

The only effective way to solve this dilemma is to make a definite mental decision to believe that God's Word, the Bible, is God's revealed truth to the world and therefore to you. The Bible assures you this is in fact true:

> *All Scripture is given by inspiration of God, and is profit-*
> *able for doctrine, for reproof, for correction, for instruc-*
> *tion in righteousness, that the man of God may be*
> *complete, thoroughly equipped for every good work.*
> —2 TIMOTHY 3:16

God's Word is reliable for giving you wisdom regarding life issues, to help you choose the correct path, to know the difference between right and wrong, to prompt you when you go astray, and to help you become the person you were born to be, fulfilling your destiny.

The Bible reveals that God's Word has an inherent power when wielded by the Holy Spirit. You will not only be led into truth and given the wisdom and insight you so desperately need but you will also be given the ability to discern fundamental motivations.

> *For the word of God is living and powerful, and sharper*
> *than any two-edged sword, piercing even to the division*
> *of soul and spirit, and of joints and marrow, and is a dis-*
> *cerner of the thoughts and intents of the heart.*
> —HEBREWS 4:12

Through studying God's Word you are empowered on the inside helping you see the difference between the workings of your soul and the Spirit. Cutting between these two will bring revelation as to what is of God, what is of Satan, and what is of your flesh. Availing yourself of this powerful gift will greatly reduce confusion in your life.

Once you have decided to believe that God's Word is His truth, it is time to put this belief into action. Read your Bible daily, starting today, and fill your mind with its truth. Study it deeply so you gain knowledge of who God really is and the wisdom you need to navigate your circumstances. God wants to help you. Jesus says, "Without Me you can do nothing" (John 15:5), and in this statement He is including being set free from anxiety. However, He also says, "If you abide in Me, and My words abide in you, you will ask what you desire, and it shall be done for you" (John 15:7). His words are contained in His Bible; and He says if these words abide in you—in other words if they are established in your heart and you are living them—then you are in a position to be set free and receive His blessing. Anxiety is not part of His plan for you. Overcoming doubt will lead to overcoming anxiety.

UNBELIEF

Unbelief is a child of doubt. When you constantly doubt truth, then in your mind it is not sensible to believe anything. However, when doubt is eliminated by a decision to accept God's Word as truth, then unbelief can be reserved for untruths that are not contained within the Bible.

Unbelief of biblical truth has serious consequences. It limits God's power to work miracles. In Nazareth Jesus "did not do many mighty works there because of their unbelief" (Matt. 13:58). Not only can you miss God's miraculous power manifesting in your life, but if unbelief is not dealt with firmly, it will eventually steal your faith and "without faith it is impossible to please [God]" (Heb. 11:6). Unbelief will also keep you in a state of turmoil hijacking your ability to enter into God's rest, preventing you from overcoming your problem with anxiety. The Israelites suffered this way: "They could not enter [His rest] because of unbelief" (Heb. 3:19).

Having a problem with unbelief is not uncommon. Even the disciples suffered this way when they heard that Christ had risen from the dead and had not yet seen Him with their eyes. When Jesus "appeared to the eleven as they sat at the table...He rebuked their unbelief and hardness of heart, because they did not believe those who had seen Him after He had risen" (Mark 16:14). You no longer have their excuse because although you may not have seen Christ with your physical eyes, you do have many written accounts in the Bible of those who have. Jesus' disciples didn't have this witness. You also now have the indwelling Holy Spirit who is given as a guarantee that your faith is real (2 Cor. 1:22; 2 Cor. 5:5). There is no longer any excuse for unbelief. In the above scripture Jesus also links unbelief with hardness of heart. At a deep level you are refusing to be open to God with your whole heart. You are not seeking His kingdom and His righteousness first (Matt. 6:33).

If you have trouble in this area, now is the time to repent of your unbelief to prevent it from stealing your faith and rest. And God is gracious, He knows your difficulty. Just as He healed the beloved deaf and dumb son of the father who came to Him grieving in his honesty, "Lord, I believe; help my unbelief" (Mark 9:24), so He will heal you.

SELF-PITY

Holding a "pity party" and wallowing in self-pity is a lonely experience because you are usually the only one present. No one wants to join you, at least not for long. Self-pity is a self-indulgent sin. You can see this through Jesus' response to Peter when he tried to sympathize with Jesus by suggesting He should not fulfill His destiny and die on the cross. Jesus replied, "Get behind Me, Satan! You are an offence to Me, for you are not mindful of the things of God, but the things of men" (Matt. 16:23). This interaction reveals the potential problem when well-meaning people sympathize with your anxieties. They may be backing the wrong side. As in Jesus' case, the events in your life causing your anxiety may be God's precise will for your life. He may be allowing them in order to prompt you to deal with issues you have been trying to avoid, to assist you in facing reality. It helps to remember that Jesus suffered according to God's will. So did His disciples. Paul had a remarkable tale of shipwrecks, stonings, lashings, sleeplessness, and all manner of perils (2 Cor. 11:25–27); so why would you be any different? Why should you be exempt from problems? Have you suffered to the extent Paul or Jesus did?

Self-pity is an extravagance that can lead to despair and isolation. It negates the truth that Christ is your Shepherd and that He cares for you. Yes, He may take you through the valley of the shadow of death on the way to your destination, but He promises to accompany you on the journey. When King David walked through this valley, he declared "Yea, though I walk through the valley of the shadow of death, I will fear no evil; For You [God] are with me; Your rod and Your staff, they comfort me" (Ps. 23:4). He knew he was not alone. The path was painful but he chose not to fear. Jesus says, "I am the good shepherd. The good shepherd gives His life for the sheep" (John 10:11). This is how much God cares. Jesus fulfilled His word and gave His life for you.

God also promises you will not be tempted beyond what you are able to cope with—with His help. Remember:

> *No temptation has overtaken you except such as is common to man; but God is faithful, who will not allow you to be tempted beyond what you are able, but with the temptation will also make the way of escape, that you may be able to bear it.*
> —1 CORINTHIANS 10:13

One of your ways of escape is to avoid self-pity. It is a trap. As John MacArthur advises in his book *Anxious for Nothing*, "Put a check on the complaints you utter, you will succeed in attacking anxiety at its source. You will be affirming that God knows what He is doing in your life."[2]

DOUBLE-MINDEDNESS

Doubt also breeds double-mindedness. The Bible reveals this in James 1:5–8, stating that when a man succumbs to doubt he is "a double-minded man, unstable in all his ways." He leaps between one opinion and another having nothing to anchor his belief on. The solution for this problem is the same as for doubt. You need to choose to believe the Bible is the Word of God and act accordingly by faith basing your decisions on the foundation of who Christ is as your Rock.

Of course, not every detail for every event in life is stated clearly in the Bible. You are not told who to marry or which university to attend. This is where you need to use discernment and pray believing God will lead you. Why? Simply because He is God, He knows the future, He has a plan for your life, He loves you, and He says He will lead you. Double-mindedness develops because you are not sure what you want to believe or who you want to believe. The scriptural antidote for double-mindedness is to purify your heart (James 4:8). As you sincerely come before God in repentance willing your heart to be cleansed, your double-mindedness will vanish.

EXCUSES

When you fail miserably or don't reach your expectations, the temptation is to make excuses and justify your actions or thoughts. When your reasoning leads to blaming others for circumstances or anything except taking responsibility yourself, this is called projection. Projection traps you in your present condition. Many people spend their entire lives here, locked in their refusal to face truth. Of course, it is possible that others may have sinned against you, but you are still responsible for how you respond.

Excuses and projection may satisfy friends and family for a time, but they never work with God. He always knows the truth. He is never fooled. He always knows exactly what your motivation for any thought or action is or was in the past. Because He knows the truth, He wants to lead you into this truth also so that you can find healing and resolve your problems. It is time to stop making excuses and blaming everyone around you or even your past. In the end the only person you are fooling is yourself. Let's face it, even most of your friends can see through your weak pretense. God wants you to be real. This is the only way you will move forward and be set free. If you decide to respond in a Christ-like manner, God will help you overcome no matter how bad the situation appears.

BARGAINING

Before you are prepared to humbly submit to God's will, you may find yourself bargaining with Him: "God, if you will help me stop being anxious then I promise I will read your Word every day!" The problem is, you still want life on your terms. You still want to maintain control. However, God's kingdom has only one King and He is the King of all kings, God Himself; and He wants you to deeply understand His sovereignty. Even when God occasionally, graciously does listen to your immature conditions, it is very rare you will keep them. As soon as life once again goes in your desired direction, the deal is off!

In reality, you are in no position to bargain with God. You are the creature not the Creator. You are subject to His mercy. And God is gracious. He does not expect you to be faultless. He knows your faults; and He is in the process of helping you change, heal, and grow in every area of your life, emotionally, mentally, and spiritually into the likeness of His Son, Jesus Christ. You need to be honest with yourself, God, and others to allow this process to progress and succeed. The more honest you are, the faster your growth will be.

DISTRACTIONS

Distractions are the last "little foxes" we will ferret out of the vines. They can be used to avoid dealing with important issues in your life. Distractions may appear to be urgent, but in reality they are not. Instead, they keep you away from doing the real work you need to do in your life. They can take many guises coming in the form of friends, socializing, watching television, talking on the phone, using the Internet, reading novels, gossiping, and even exercising. You are very resourceful! It's not hard to think up reasons why you can't do the hard work in your life of facing truth, confronting evil, repenting, and grieving losses. However, if you want to be set free from anxiety and experience the rest and freedom Christ died to give you, then you will need to take time alone with God and look at the areas He wants you to examine. I am sure you are already aware of many of these.

∞

The basic problem behind these seven little foxes or thinking and behavior traps is that they rely on sight instead of faith. You are told that "the just shall live by his faith" (Hab. 2:4) and "without faith it is impossible to please [God]" (Heb. 11:6), so let's take a moment and discover what real faith looks like.

Hebrews 11:1 says, "Faith is the substance of things hoped for, the evidence of things not seen." This verse reveals that faith is not a wishy-washy aberration based on nothing. Instead it has definite "substance," even though this substance may be invisible because it is "not seen." So what is this substance? I believe it is everything the Bible reveals about who God is, what His character is like, how He works, and what He says. Your faith needs to be built on who God really is for you to be able to walk in faith victoriously.

The only effective starting place for this knowledge and understanding is once again humbly reading God's Word, reflecting your insights and thoughts in prayer, and developing a personal relationship with Him. From this foundation you can learn to know who God is and what He is like, not only initially through your reading and revelation from the Holy Spirit but also through the personal experience of walking with Him through life. "Jesus [is] the author and the finisher of our faith" (Heb. 12:2). Regardless of what you may be going through in life right now, the writer of Hebrews suggests your life will only fall into perspective as you do the following:

> *Consider Him who endured such hostility from sinners against Himself, lest you become weary and discouraged in your souls. You have not yet resisted to bloodshed, striving against sin. And you have forgotten the exhortation which speaks to you as to sons: My son, do not despise the chastening of the LORD, Nor be discouraged when you are rebuked by Him; For whom the LORD loves He chastens, And scourges every son whom He receives.*
> —HEBREWS 12:3–6

As you go through difficult times, including your problem with anxiety, realize God is with you and He loves you. Dwell on this. He is in the process of changing you so that you may be a partaker of "His holiness" (v. 10). And although the process may not feel like fun, if you stick with it, afterwards you will feel "the peaceable fruit of righteousness to those who have been trained by it" (v. 11). This peaceable fruit is a place far from the tyranny of anxiety. Real progress requires a deepening of your relationship with God. Let's move forward now and explore how this develops.

GETTING REAL

Which "little foxes" have I allowed to interfere with my relationship with God?

Write them down and beside each write the issues they relate to: For example:

Unbelief: I don't believe God is good.

Double-mindedness: I'm not sure I really want to surrender my right to myself.

Pray over each item and ask God for wisdom so you can understand what He wants you to do about them. Write down what you think God is saying.

How can I begin to do what I believe God is saying? What is my first step?

What is stopping me?

Do I spend regular time alone with God? Am I willing to begin spending more time alone with Him? If the answer is yes, then keep a journal and write down what is happening for you and what you think God is saying.

Chapter Seven

GOD'S SPACE

The only way to know God is to do His will.
—ANDREW MURRAY[1]

GOD INVITES YOU to come into His space and get to know Him.

> *He has made from one blood every nation of men to dwell on the face of the earth, and has determined their pre-appointed times and the boundaries of their dwellings, so that they should seek the Lord, in the hope that they might grope for Him and find Him, though He is not far from each of us; for in Him we live and move and have our being.*
> —ACTS 17:26–28

It is through knowing God that you come to experience the abundant life Christ died to give you. Jesus says, "I have come that they may have life, and that they may have it more abundantly" (John 10:10). And He doesn't leave you stranded to find out how to do this. He also says, "No one knows the Son except the Father, and no one knows the Father except the Son and anyone to whom the Son chooses to reveal him" (Matt. 11:27, ESV).

The kind of knowing you need that will really help does not come solely through human effort and wisdom. It is a revelation from Christ Himself and requires a personal relationship with God. In this relationship you can talk with Him, praise Him, rejoice with Him, listen to Him, and be aware that He personally lives with you, within you, to bless you (John 14:23); and from there you will obey Him.

As you grow in your relationship with God, it may seem rather strange at times because God says, "For as the heavens are higher than the earth, So are My ways higher than your ways, And My thoughts than your thoughts" (Isa. 55:9). It can take a little while to catch on to some of His ways. In fact, it might take a lifetime. But what an adventure!

God promises that, regardless of where you start, "from there you will seek the LORD your God, and you will find Him if you seek Him with all your heart and with all your soul" (Deut. 4:29). It is your whole self that needs to be involved. Not just a part of you. God invites you into His spiritual space and He wants you to enjoy the experience.

> *Let not the wise man boast in his wisdom, let not the mighty man boast in his might, let not the rich man boast in his riches, but let him who boasts boast in this, that he understands and knows me, that I am the LORD who practices steadfast love, justice, and righteousness in the earth. For in these things I delight, declares the LORD.*
> —JEREMIAH 9:23–24, ESV

God is close. He says He is available to know. He is full of compassion and has given you many ways to be with Him. Let's briefly explore four of these: prayer, the Word, the Spirit, and praise.

PRAYER

Prayer is the antibiotic for anxiety. You are commanded:

> *Be anxious for nothing, but in everything by prayer and supplication, with thanksgiving, let your requests be made known to God; and the peace of God, which surpasses all understanding, will guard your hearts and minds through Christ Jesus.*
> —PHILIPPIANS 4:6–7

If you come with a repentant heart and pray to the all-knowing, all-wise God who is love (as He is described in the Bible), you can know that your requests are heard and treasured (Luke 11:9). And when He decides the time is right, He will send you His answer. All sincere prayer is answered. It's just that sometimes the answer may come in a package you least expect. And it may not be the answer you thought you wanted. However, God in His wisdom knows what is best for you in the long term. He sees all of time and knows every fact, whereas you can only see what you think is real and you have no idea what may transpire in the future. There will always be factors you are not aware of that need to be considered in the overall outcome of your situation. And usually God will not reveal His complete will for your life all at once. Right now you will only see part of the whole but when all the pieces fall into place, God's way will not seem so strange.

Once you have given your requests to God, you no longer need to hang on to them, twirling them around in your mind. Remember, God knows the best answer. He knows everything and is in control so you can safely leave your requests with Him. The disciple Peter says to "humble yourself under the mighty hand of God, that He may exalt you in due time, casting all your care upon Him, for He cares for you" (1 Pet. 5:7). If you do, you will soon discover that in place of your concerns He gives you an amazing depth of peace that does not originate in this world. It is a supernatural gift from His kingdom. We will look more into this in a later chapter but for now your work is to pray. Resist phoning a friend first; pray first. Write your prayer in your journal and record the answer when it comes. God doesn't need you to write it down but you may, to help you remember and to encourage you while you get used to the idea that God is very responsible with your prayers.

The only time God says He will not listen is if you are knowingly walking in sin. "Now we know that God does not hear sinners; but if anyone is a worshiper of God and does His will, He hears him" (John 9:31). Obedience, doing what you know is right, is essential. The apostle James says, "He who...is not a forgetful hearer but a doer of the work, this one will be blessed in what he does" (James 1:25). James also points out the importance of motives when bringing your requests to God. You are unlikely to receive an answer to prayer when your motives are impure. Be sure your request is not solely for your own pleasures (James 4:3) and is in line with God's will.

The Word

We have already spoken about the Word of God. You must believe it is God's inspired Word containing His truth. Through obeying what the Bible says, you will discover that power comes into your life to gradually transform you. "Do not be conformed to this world, but be transformed by the renewing of your mind, that you may prove what is the good and acceptable and perfect will of God" (Rom. 12:2). As your mind is renewed and you come to know God's will, you will no longer have anything to worry about. Through reading Scripture daily your faith will grow. "Faith comes by hearing, and hearing by the word of God" (Rom. 10:17). And as your faith grows you will begin to trust God more. And so the cycle continues out of anxiety and into His wonderful peace.

The Holy Spirit

We have also looked briefly at the work of the Holy Spirit. He plays a vital role in your communication with God; and as you experience more of His work in your life, you will gradually learn to trust your experiences with Him. He is God dwelling within your spirit. He leads you into truth so that you can understand what He is saying. "When He, the Spirit of truth has come, He will guide you into all truth; for He will not speak on His own authority, but whatever He hears He will speak; and He will tell you things to come" (John 16:13). He helps you remember what God has done for you in the past (John 14:26). He teaches you (vv. 26; 16:13) and manifests spiritual gifts from within to help you obey and succeed (Acts 2:4; 1 Cor. 12). He reveals visions of the future (John 16:13) and points out areas of ministry and service (Acts 16:6; Rom 7:6). And He reveals God's love and hope to you (Rom. 5:5). The Holy Spirit gives you His power, released within your spirit, to overcome your fears and fulfill the plans God has for your life. The fruit of His life within reveals itself outwardly as you receive His power; and you will notice yourself changing and growing in your capacity to love and experience joy, peace, long-suffering, kindness, goodness, faithfulness, gentleness, and self-control (Gal. 5:22). All of these are necessary to overcome your anxious thoughts.

PRAISE

You are commanded, "Rejoice in the Lord always. Again I will say, rejoice!" (Phil. 4:4). And when Philippians 4:6–7 says to be anxious for nothing and bring all your requests to God, you are asked to bring them with thanksgiving. Praise eliminates self-pity and doubt. When praising God, your mind is not focused on yourself and your problems. Praise builds faith and belief as you reflect on the wonderful character and attributes of God and magnify His holiness, perfection, grace, love, kindness, wisdom, endless knowledge, and guidance. Praise works, even when times are difficult and the effort feels like a tremendous sacrifice. "Therefore by Him let us continually offer the sacrifice of praise to God, that is the fruit of our lips, giving thanks to His name" (Heb. 13:15). A good example of this is in Acts 5:40–41, when the apostles rejoiced after being unfairly beaten. In the beginning you may feel like gritting your teeth; but once the words begin to flow, they penetrate your mind and spirit, and your heart will gradually open to the truths you are vocalizing. Your spirit will then rise to meet with Him in sincerity and love; and before you are fully aware, you will be soaring in your Father's heavenly presence.

⸎

God invites you to come into His spiritual space to be with Him. He loves you and wants to spend precious time with you. He wants to set you free from anxiety so you can enjoy the abundant life He has planned for you, and so that you can walk in the freedom Christ died to give you. As Andrew Murray so aptly says, "He who seeks to live with God will learn to know His mind and to please Him, so that he will be able to pray according to His will."[2] In this place, in His spiritual space praying according to His will, you can know you are heard and what you ask will be done. In such a position anxiety will flee and praise will freely flow from you. However, to maintain this position requires vital, consistent choices.

GETTING REAL

How often do I enter God's space to be with Him?

Because He is interested in every intimate area of my life, what else can I share with Him in truth?

Do I regularly read my Bible?

Am I learning about God as I read my Bible? If not, will I consider using a study guide or concordance or reading books to discover more about who He is and how He works?[3]

How deeply am I allowing the Holy Spirit to be actively involved in my life? How well do I know who He is and how He works?

What situations do I praise God in? Do I praise Him in difficult times?

When can I praise Him more?

Chapter Eight

CHOICES

*We are right when, and only when, we stand in a
right position relative to God, and we are wrong so
far and so long as we stand in any other position.*
—A.W. TOZER[1]

GOD MADE YOU with the ability to choose. He made this very
clear when He spoke to the Israelites giving them the choice
between blessings and curses. He gives you the same opportunity to choose. He makes it so easy He even gives the answer:

*I have set before you life and death, blessing and cursing;
therefore choose life, that both you and your descendants
may live; that you may love the LORD your God, that you
may obey His voice, and that you may cling to Him, for
He is your life and the length of your days.*
—DEUTERONOMY 30:19–20

What are you choosing now? What have you been choosing in
the past? What do you want to choose in the future?

The result of choosing correctly—life—includes choosing
blessing for yourself, your children, and grandchildren; and it
includes the ability to love God from the depths of your heart,
tapping into the fountain of love He pours into your heart (Rom.
5:5). It is out of a response to this love, poured into your heart,
that you will be able to make wise choices and obey God. Jesus
says, "If you love Me, keep My commandments" (John 14:15).
Love results in obedience because out of love for God you will
actually *want* to obey Him. It won't be a burden. Instead it will
become your heart's desire. Of course this doesn't mean it will

always be easy, as anything worthwhile goes through periods of difficulty. Choosing life means you will grow to know God more and understand His importance in every facet of life. Your heart will be expanded and your eyes opened so that you will want to cling to Him because you will know deep inside that He is the source of life. The blessings from choosing correctly are multiplied eternally.

However, if you choose incorrectly, you will also experience consequences; and as the passage in Deuteronomy says, your choice will lead to death. This may not mean physical death instantly but it will mean spiritual death. And this death will ooze like a pus-filled, running sore into your relationships, work, and soul. As with the choice of life, the choice of death permeates every facet of life, and darkness and decay will spread extensively. Paul says that those who "did not like to retain God in their knowledge, God gave them over to a debased mind, to do those things which are not fitting" (Rom. 1:28). Even your thinking will dramatically change.

Clearly there are severe consequences following any choice you make. What are you choosing when you choose to worry? Are you choosing life or death? Does anxiety add positive elements to your life or take away from your life? As Proverbs 12:25 reveals, when left unchecked anxiety resulting from wrong choices can lead down the dark road to depression.

It is clear that choosing anxiety is choosing death because Jesus clearly states that if you are following Him, seeking His kingdom and righteousness first, then there is no need to worry about anything. And He tells you why: "Seek first the kingdom of God and His righteousness, and all these things shall be added to you" (Matt. 6:33). The "all these things" that are added as a result of doing life His way includes everything you will ever need to accomplish His will. When you choose to worry and be anxious, you are side-stepping God; and instead of relying on Him to help solve your problems, you are turning to yourself or looking elsewhere for answers. Are you more capable of solving your problems than God? Are you equal to Him in knowledge, understanding, wisdom, perfection, and power? Is anyone else you know?

There is much good advice in the world; but the problem with relying on other people to solve your problems, no matter how skilled they are, is that they do not have the resources God has at His disposal. They do not possess His perfect character. They cannot see into the future. And if you look at their lives, it also becomes clear they have enough trouble solving their own problems!

The problem with relying on yourself instead of God is that from experience you already know you do not have all the answers. You know deep inside you are incapable of solving all your dilemmas. You don't even have all the information. You don't know all the details. You don't have the wisdom. You don't know the future. And you don't know what other people's responses will be.

Perhaps it is time to face the fact that you and other people may not be the best options to find solutions to your problems and instead acknowledge your need for revelation to get to the bottom of the issues. And, of course, revelation does not come through logical thought or common sense. It only comes from God through His Holy Spirit and is usually only received as a result of a personal relationship with Him.

I say "usually" because God can choose to reveal Himself to anyone He chooses; He is not limited by anyone's belief system. He was able to make His will known to Abimelech who was about to take Abraham's wife as his own not knowing she was already married. God did not have a problem letting him know the truth in a dream even though to our knowledge he was not a believer (Gen. 20:2–6). However, if you are in relationship with Him, God wants to draw you closer into this relationship and, therefore, you need to learn to do things His way, not yours.

He tells you clearly what to do instead of relying on yourself or others. You are to "be anxious for nothing, but in everything by prayer and supplication, with thanksgiving, let your requests be known to God" (Phil. 4:6). You can choose to talk to Him through prayer, bringing all your concerns before Him so that He can answer you in His timing, instead of becoming anxious winding yourself in circles searching for answers. It is only after following God's way that you will experience His supernatural peace (v. 7).

Included in your power to choose is your ability to choose what you think about. And because thoughts result in feelings, you therefore have a level of control over how you feel in any situation. We have discussed this previously, but let's now delve more deeply into the importance of obedience.

OBEDIENCE

Obedience is not an optional extra in your walk of faith. Christ says, "If you love Me, keep my commandments" (John 14:15). However, we are not talking here about a heartless legalism. Obedience is about learning to abide in His love. Abiding takes staying power, courage, and faith. It's about dwelling in, remaining in, and being one with. Imagine a vineyard. The branches cannot decide to grow separated from the vine, and the grapes are not produced separated from the branches. In spiritual terms Jesus is your vine and you are a branch (John 15:1–8). He provides the life-giving sap to keep you alive. He is your life-giver, your provider, the lover of your soul. He is the source of all things good. He is the one who produces the fruit that will grow in your life as you remain in Him. You can't make this happen. You can't hold your breath, become frantic, anxious, plead, beg, or demand the fruit to grow. All you can do is humbly obey and abide. The consequences are up to God. Obedience leads to more abiding as you see the positive results and grow in your knowledge and understanding of God; and this abiding leads to more purposeful obedience. One of the most positive results from this cycle of choosing love, abiding, and obedience is peace of mind regardless of unusual or traumatic events raging around you. And as you continue to abide and obey, leaving the consequences up to God, you will discover you are learning to trust.

As your trust in Jesus grows more and more, you will again

yearn to increase your obedience—because obedience starts to make serious sense. And as you obey, your love will continue to grow and it will be accompanied by joy—because finally you begin to see the bountiful fruit of your obedience and it is truly good. And so this renewed love leads once again to more obedience on an upward cycle, going deeper and deeper into relationship with God. This is why if you love Him you will be able to keep His commandments because you will be abiding in His love. He will be at the center, the anchor of your heart.

Every choice you make will either take you closer to God or further away from Him. If you stop for a moment and deeply consider, you will know which way you are going. When a pilot is only a few degrees off course and does not correct his position, in just a few hours he will miss his destination by hundreds of miles. The choice is up to you. God will nudge you, convicting you by the Holy Spirit; but the decision is yours.

GETTING REAL

Am I abiding in Christ?

How can I know?

Am I moving toward God or further away from Him?

What do I need to change to turn back in the right direction in any area of my life?

Am I prepared to make the changes I need to make?

What are these changes?

How and when will I make them?

Chapter Nine

POWER HOUSE

Power belongs to God.

He rules by His power forever.
—Psalms 62:11; 66:7

If you decide to make good choices and are prepared to change, the question needs to be asked: How can this happen? The answer, of course, lies in the above biblical quotes. The power necessary to change does not originate in you, it originates in God. He is the foundational source of all power.

> *Yours, O Lord, is the greatness, The power and the glory, The victory and majesty; For all that is in heaven and in earth is Yours; Yours is the kingdom, O Lord, And You are exalted as head over all.*
> —1 Chronicles 29:11

Accepting this, you must discover how to avail yourself of this power so you can receive it into your life and effectively change. After this, your part is to willingly cooperate.

Change is never easy because we seem to naturally resist whatever is new; and the older we become, the more set in our ways we tend to be. However, God has a great antidote for this mindset. He says, "Whoever does not receive the kingdom of God as a little child will by no means enter it" (Mark 10:15). What is it about little children that endears them to God's kingdom?

Children are always curious. They explore everything. They don't even think about danger when their parents are around.

They ask endless questions. They trust implicitly. They thrive in their innocence. They are teachable. They are delightfully mischievous! They love openly and unconditionally—and nothing seems impossible! Do any of these characteristics describe you in your relationship with God?

Somewhere along the avenue of life we lose much of our spontaneity. Yet God wants to refresh you and dust off this sleeping child within. This little person is still resident deep inside, hiding in the shadows of your soul; even if he is smothered in layers of dust and encased in stiff old-fashioned clothes, even if his ability to laugh and linger seems to have long been forgotten. It is time to unveil your child's sweet innocence and joyful freedom, to rediscover the wonders of life, and to dare to begin to trust again under the protection of your powerful God.

However, this joyful lost little child may not be the only youngster slinking in the dark shadows of your soul. Perhaps his twin is cowering in shrouds of fear, too frightened or too shy to speak and become all he was meant to be. Perhaps he (or she) has been emotionally, physically, or sexually abused and is far too timid to venture out toward the light.

Consider for a moment what the long term results will be if you do not address painful issues from your past. You are unlikely to deeply change for good. Instead, you are likely to become more encased in your prison of pain and anxiety. Perhaps now it is time to whisper in your small child's ear the words of the apostle Paul: "If anyone is in Christ, he is a new creation; old things have passed away; behold, all things have become new" (2 Cor. 5:17). This newness is provided under God's powerful sovereignty.

God says you are a "new creation"—the old has gone away and the brand-new has come. This is a reality if you are a child of God. Children love new things. They love to explore and enjoy them in an environment where they feel safe. In terms of spiritual growth, this newness does not mean losing your personality, talents, or identity, or even your memories, as these are attributes God created you with and the circumstances that have shaped you into the person you are today. Instead, it means you can slip off your independent individuality that seeks its identity outside of God and has brought you into the fearful anxious state you are in today. In its place you can gain all the fullness of who you were created to be. To accomplish this you will need to have Christ's own disposition transplanted within you.

Open your heart today and ask God to do this work that only He can do within your spirit. This is your redemption. As Oswald Chambers reveals, "The moral miracle of Redemption is that God can put into me a new disposition whereby I can live a totally new life. When I reach the frontier of need and know my limitations, Jesus says 'Blessed are you.' But I have to get there. God cannot put into me, a responsible moral being, the disposition that was in Jesus Christ unless I am conscious I need it."[1] Are you conscious that you need to change deeply on the inside? If so, ask Jesus to help you. This is where the power to change comes from. It is not something you are capable of doing alone by trying harder, worrying more, or condemning yourself. It is a gift from God.

As you trust in the work Christ accomplished on the cross, He says your old sinful disposition that was inherited from Adam and steers toward the negative has died with Him so that now you can live in resurrection life. This new form of life, as we have seen, is supplied by Him. You don't need to invent it. And this life is abundant. It is a life of freedom and peace. He says, "If the Son makes you free, you shall be free indeed" (John 8:36). This new life and freedom are gifts Christ has the power to give, as you believe and abide in Him.

To experience the fulfillment of these truths requires the death of your self, your old life, and a taking up and receiving of the new. We will explore the process of doing this in the next chapters, but for now it is important to remember that the power to accomplish this transforming change does not come from you. It comes from God (Ps. 62:11). It doesn't matter how weak you think you are. He strengthens the weak. "He gives power to the weak, And to those who have no might He increases strength" (Isa. 40:29). He will even give you the power to be willing to receive His help if you are too fearful to begin: "For it is God who works in you both to will and do His good pleasure" (Phil. 2:13).

It makes no difference what state your little child within is in today. Is she sleeping hidden under the covers? Is she playing peek-a-boo behind thick velvet curtains? Has he turned into a monster? Does he scream and shout and demand his own way? God is bigger than all these aberrations. He is the Lord of lords, the King of kings, your mighty powerful God who also embodies the heart of the gentlest mother. He cried out to the Israelites: "How often I wanted to gather your children together, as a hen gathers her chicks under her wings, but you were not willing!" (Matt. 23:37). You can be willing today. Are you willing to dare to receive your gifts from God?

Once you accept God's gift of new life and leave the dead old self, the body of sin, and your past behind, God empowers you from within enabling you to live the way He wants you to. This power comes from His Holy Spirit dwelling inside you. As you receive the baptism of the Holy Spirit and allow Him to work in His strength through you, He will guide you into your new life of freedom and peace.

You will always have the ongoing choice of listening to what He says, of abiding and obeying, or of refusing to listen and going back to your old ways; God is a gentleman. He will never make you do anything. He gives you the choice, but if you refuse to do things His way—and remember He only ever wants what is best for you—you will suffer the consequences of your choices. Psalm 81:11–12 reveals this in God's dealings with the Israelites: "My people would not heed My voice....So I gave them over to their own stubborn heart, To walk in their own counsels." Their own counsels were places far from God's presence where instead of experiencing fulfillment and peace, they encountered pain and dismay. Obedience is a far more rewarding choice.

One of the most amazing benefits of choosing God's way and following the directions of the Holy Spirit is that with each correct choice you will experience greater freedom (John 8:32). Your child within can venture into the sunshine, able to dance and play. This path of freedom leads away from the bondage to anxiety. It leads away from the tyranny of compulsive fear-filled thoughts, apprehension, uneasiness, and perplexity. One choice at a time is all it takes, one choice each moment in the right direction—your hand stretched out toward your heavenly Father rather than turning away from Him. If your heart is willing and longing for this to be real in your life, let's continue on our journey into a deeper revelation of change.

GETTING REAL

Am I willing to reach out my hand and receive my new resurrection life from God?

Am I willing to be changed from the inside out?

Am I willing to begin to move toward God with every choice I make?

Is anything stopping me? If so, what is it?

Why is this stopping me?

Am I baptized in the Holy Spirit? Am I willing to be? If so, ask God for this gift now. (If you are unsure read about this experience in the Book of Acts.)

If you have difficulty daring to be willing, perhaps you will be more willing if you could only believe. We will look at this in the next chapter.

Chapter Ten

BELIEVING

*Whatever a heart truly believes, it receives
and allows to master and rule the life.*
—ANDREW MURRAY[1]

IF ONLY YOU could truly believe! If only you could believe it really was that easy for God to change your life! You have tried to change for so long. You have tried so hard to give up your anxiety. But it hasn't worked, has it? Otherwise you wouldn't be reading this book. Why do you think it hasn't worked?

It may be because your emotions still tie you to your old ways. You hear something, watch something, think something, and all those old emotions come rushing back and flood your world with fear. Your heart beats faster, your palms sweat, and you look about frantically for something to divert your attention, to try and stop the vicious cycle.

Whenever you experience an emotion, and it doesn't matter what this emotion is, you can be sure it is preceded by a thought even if you have not consciously linked the two. Imagine for a moment two people, each phoning a friend on their cell phone and the friend doesn't answer. One feels annoyed and the other anxious. Why? They are both experiencing the same event and yet they are feeling completely different emotions. Perhaps the annoyed woman believes her friend is avoiding her and doesn't want to answer the phone, or perhaps she is annoyed because she feels she has wasted some of her time! The anxious one, on the other hand, may believe something terrible has happened to her friend so she is not able to answer her phone. The same event but what different responses and results!

As Andrew Murray points out in the quote beginning this chapter, whatever you truly believe deep in your heart will result in your actions and feelings. So let's get deeply personal for a moment. What do you truly believe? Do you really believe God is able and capable to be trusted to run the universe? Do you really believe He has the power to run it the way He wants? Do you really believe God loves you in spite of your faults and that He wants good things for your life? Do you believe He is powerful enough to influence your life for good? And that He wants to? You need to be very honest here; because the truth is, if you really do believe these things, you will never have any need to be anxious again!

If you have a problem with anxiety, in all honesty you must face the fact that you do not actually believe many or all of these truths about God. Or perhaps there are other truths about Him you are struggling to believe. The first three chapters of this book have attempted to resolve these issues; but if you have not, then study the Word of God yourself and read books on relevant topics to help you come to the place where you do believe the truth contained in the Bible.

It can sometimes take years to truly resolve some of these issues in your heart. As long as they are unresolved, they will rule your thinking, feelings, and behavior and undermine your relationship with God and the freedom you experience. Now is the time to seriously begin to confront these issues. Are you going to believe God is good and that He rewards those who diligently seek Him (Heb. 11:6)? The Bible says He does!

He also says, "I will never leave nor forsake you" (Heb. 13:5). And He tells you, "God so loved the world [*this means you*] that He gave His only begotten Son, that whoever believes in Him [*this means you*] should not perish but have everlasting life (John 3:16). This everlasting life is the supernatural abundant life He longs to give you.

He says, "I know the thoughts that I think toward you, says the LORD, thoughts of peace and not of evil, to give you a future and a hope" (Jer. 29:11). And He tells you that nothing and no one can separate you from the love of Christ. Not tribulation, distress, persecution, famine, nakedness, peril, or even a sword pointed at your belly (Rom. 8:35). And He knows your deepest thoughts and feelings even when you wish to keep them secret (Ps. 139:1–2). So why not be open and honest with Him?

"As for God, His way is perfect; The word of the LORD is proven; He is a shield to all who trust in Him" (Ps. 18:30). And underlying it all is this: "God is love" (1 John 4:8). And His love is pure.

All of the above statements are true. They are God's love messages to you personally. Dwell on them. Meditate on them. Ponder them deeply. Open your heart and receive them inside the raw broken parts of you, those places that have been deeply damaged by people and events in the past. And remember, God says, "*He* heals the brokenhearted and binds up their wounds" (Ps. 147:3, emphasis added). No one else can do this for you. Only God has the power to deliver on this promise!

Now dwell on messages Jesus gives you:

- "I am the light of the world. He who follows Me shall not walk in darkness, but have the light of life" (John 8:12).

- "I am the true vine" (John 15:1).

- "I am the good shepherd" (John 10:11).

- "I am the door of the sheep" (John 10:7).

- "I am good" (Matt. 20:15).

- "I am the resurrection and the life" (John 11:25).

- "I am with you always, even to the end of the age" (Matt. 28:20).

- "I am the bread of life" (John 6:35).

- "I am the way, the truth, and the life. No one comes to the Father except through Me" (John 14:6).

Jesus says that if you come to Him you will never hunger and if you believe in Him you will never thirst (John 6:35). To believe in Him means to believe what He says is true. Coming to Him is your food, you need this to survive; but you also need to believe what He says so that you can receive what He longs to give you. If you do, your longing, your yearning, your thirst will be satisfied at its deepest point. This means your craving for security, self-worth, significance, and love will be filled to overflowing. Your search will be over and your striving ended. You will be able to come and at last tilt your head back on His heavenly shoulder, put your feet up and rest your heart, your mind, your will, and your volatile emotions as well as your spirit in Him.

If you choose to refuse to believe Jesus is who He says He is, then you will be separated from God, walking in the opposite direction, and you will die in your sins (John 8:24). It is your choice whether to believe Him or not. No one can force you to do or believe anything. What do you choose? Who do you choose to believe?

If you are still in doubt, let's now look at some truths about you. Without God you will die in your sins separated from all that is associated with Him; this means all love, light, goodness, justice, kindness, and positive power. But if you accept Him as Lord and Savior, you become part of His royal family. In this new relationship, if you choose it, who are you? And what do you need to believe about yourself in this new position? Some people find it very difficult to believe the wonderful, perfect, loving God of the universe, the eternal Creator, would bother with them at all. Yet, if you are a member of His family, this is what God says about you:

- You are a partaker of His divine nature (2 Pet. 1:4)—you are able to obey Him.

- You are called of God (2 Tim. 1:9)—He has a unique purpose for your life.

- You are being changed into His image (2 Cor. 3:18; Phil. 1:6)—you are changing, becoming all you were created to be.

- You are beloved in God (Col. 3:12; Rom. 1:7; 1 Thess. 1:4)—you are loved for who you are right now!

- You can do all things in Christ (Phil. 4:13)—nothing God asks you to do is impossible for you.

- You always triumph in Christ (2 Cor. 2:14). You are more than a conqueror through Him who loves you (Rom. 8:37)—He gives you the power to succeed.

- You are a new creature (2 Cor. 5:17)—the past no longer has power over you.

And this is only the beginning. The truths of who God is and how mighty He is fill the Testaments, and the truths about who you are in Christ spill in abundance from the pages. There is enough treasure contained within the Bible to keep you exploring, digging, and receiving for a lifetime. However, you may still be thinking: *I know the words, I have read them, but somewhere in my heart I still do not believe them. What can I do?* Try this:

- Dig for the treasure.

- Savor it, dwell upon it, and turn it over in your mind.

- Keep dwelling on it.

- See how it relates to your life.

- Confess it out loud.

- Tell someone about it.

- Ask God to help you experience the truth more fully in your daily life.

- Thank God for His blessings and revelations as
  they are revealed.

In time, as you repeat this over and over seeking to understand and know God more and more, the truth will gradually move from your head into your heart. It moves as a result of experience. In other words, as you dwell in the truth, it changes you and you experience God working in your life in tangible ways. He is always working in your life and has always been working, but perhaps you have not always recognized Him. Don't limit the ways you allow Him to communicate with you. He is an awesome God. He is endlessly creative. As Smith Wigglesworth so aptly said, "If you believe in Him, you are purified for He is pure. You are strengthened, for He is strong. You are made whole because He is whole."[2] As you spend time with Him, you change.

<u>Getting Real</u>

What truths about God am I having trouble believing?

What truths about Jesus am I having trouble believing?

What truths about myself as a Christian am I having trouble believing?

What can I do about this?

When am I going to start?

Thank God for the changes you see in your life as they are revealed. Write them in your journal.

Chapter Eleven

RECEIVING

Whoever receives Me, receives not Me but Him who sent Me.

*The things which you learned and received and
heard and saw in me [Paul], these do, and
the God of peace will be with you.*

—MARK 9:37; PHILIPPIANS 4:9

As ADULTS WE can have a serious problem receiving. We can find it hard not only to receive help from others but also difficult to receive love and even rest when these are offered. So we spend our lives protecting ourselves from people who actually might sincerely want to help us, or even love us, and from situations where we can truly be restored and changed. We remain constantly busy, cushioning ourselves from the vulnerability we would experience if we dared stop for a moment in the space that is created for real joy and rest. We are afraid of these spaces because we have not yet learned to open our hearts and receive well, even if we may have come to the decision to dare to believe.

If this describes you, the problem usually has its roots in childhood when your needs were not meet and it felt unsafe to totally relax and be yourself in the presence of others, perhaps especially your parents. Sadly, this tendency can be brought over into relationships with other adults when you grow up and ultimately even with God. It becomes a destructive force preventing you from receiving God's best.

When was the last time you truly relaxed in someone's presence? When did you last relax in your own presence in the vulnerable space this creates, turning off television, radio, and cell phone and just sitting alone in the deep, resonating silence? When was the last time you truly relaxed in God's presence? Or even just sat, giving up all striving, and simply absorbed God's love?

In his book *The Inner Voice of Love*, Henri J.M. Nouwen describes this problem well. He speaks to himself:

> *A part of you was left behind very early in life: the part that never fully completely received. It is full of fears. Meanwhile, you grew up with many survival skills. But you want yourself to be one. So you have to bring home the part of you that was left behind. That is not easy, because you have become quite a formidable person, and your fearful part does not know if it can safely dwell with you. Your grown-up self has to become very childlike—hospitable, gentle, and caring—so your anxious self can return and feel safe.*[1]

Here is the damaged residue of childhood. This fearful part that is so afraid to receive remains hidden because of the terror of being hurt again, even by your grown-up, logical self. Oh, you can be so mean to yourself! But what can you do? How can this damaged, broken part become whole again so that it dares to rejoice in the reality of life with all its ups and downs? So that it can enter into the possibility of real intimate relationship with God and others?

There is only one way. You cannot do it on your own. You are not capable. You will have to rely on another, and this is why it is so difficult because so many "others" have let you down in the past and you are scared to go here again. However, sit and ponder for a moment. I suspect at some level you do want to dare to trust and move into wholeness, otherwise you would have stopped reading this book by now. And if you had stopped reading for a while, you have now picked it up again; so you are ready. Let's venture into this new space.

God is love and He says He loves you. However, He doesn't

just say it, He does something about it so that you can actually experience it. He pours His love into your heart so you are filled with it. Romans 5:5 says: "The love of God has been poured out in [your] [heart] by the Holy Spirit who was given to [you]." Notice the verse says "was poured out"; it is in the past tense, so this amazing miracle has already happened. This pouring occurred when Christ died on the cross, for you are told, "God demonstrates His own love toward [you], in that while [you] were still [a sinner], Christ died for [you]" (v. 8). And this love was transferred into your heart by the Holy Spirit when you became a child of God and were welcomed into His family.

The damaged child within and the adult within both need to receive this love. Remember, Jesus says you need to become like a little child to receive His kingdom. "Unless you are converted and become as little children, you will by no means enter the kingdom of heaven" (Matt. 18:3). Your adult self is used to giving to others and to getting on its own terms; but now your adult self needs to humble itself and turn in childlike wonder to receive God's gift. Your adult self must bow its head in awe of your Father in heaven, humbling itself to receive.

Just like every other relationship, your relationship with God is one of giving and receiving. Think of a marriage relationship where one partner always gives and never receives. The relationship can never flow in unison and love. Think of your lungs that expel air from your body ridding it of waste and toxins. If you always breathed out and refused to breathe in, you would soon expire. Your adult self must be willing and open to receive from God on His terms, not yours. Once your adult self humbles itself, then you can turn in an attitude of simple humility and invite your little frightened child to join together in receiving. Once humbled, your adult self is not so terrifying to your inner child.

When these two parts of yourself have received God's love, they need to accept this love with gratitude and love each other with God's own love. God pours His own kind of love into you, not the distorted kind you may have received as a child from an imperfect adult. God's own love, poured into your heart till it overflows, will overcome any fear that is still based in childhood experiences and will give you the strength and hope to help you grow up on the inside so that you can become one. Released at last, you will feel united within and secure in God's love. Only from here are you in a position to extend this love, God's kind of love, outward to others to love them well.

It all begins with receiving what Christ died to give you. He spilt His blood to give you His love. He died so you can receive it. As you receive His wonderful cleansing love—yielding to it, surrendering to it—the end result will be peace. Paul spoke of this union that occurs through Christ's work when writing about the union between Jews and the Gentiles. This same principle is equally true for relationships between two people and even the two sides within you.

> *For He Himself is our peace, who has made both one, and has broken down the middle wall of separation, having abolished in His flesh the enmity...so as to create in Himself one new man from the two, thus making peace.*
> —EPHESIANS 2:14–15

For this wonderful peace to become real in your experience you must not only receive His love but also His mercy, grace, and the gift of faith He wishes to give you. It is because of His mercy that He even looks on you with love and sent His Son to die to give you freedom. His grace is the means by which He gives all His gifts—it flows in endless blessing, providing you with everything you need to fulfill His will. And it is with your faith that you receive these wonderful gifts. Yet even faith is also a gift from God: "For by grace you have been saved through faith, and that not of yourselves, it is the gift of God" (Eph. 2:8). You will discover your faith increases as you walk in obedience and love, changing your actions as a result of your beliefs (Gal. 5:6).

Once you receive God's mercy, grace, and love by faith, you will begin to experience the new depth of peace you are yearning for. This is God's own peace. Jesus is your "Prince of Peace" (Isa.

9:6). This peace surpasses all human understanding. People will marvel when they know what you are going through and see and sense the supernatural peace of God that overcomes your circumstances. In Philippians 4:9, Paul says, "The things you have learned and received and heard and seen in me—practice these things, and the God of peace will be with you" (ESV). He was referring to an actual outflow into everyday life. Paul walked with "the mind of Christ"; he endeavored through Christ's strength given by the Holy Spirit to walk in the Spirit at all times. Andrew Murray reminds you: "To the degree [your] heart is given to Him in faith and [your] will is given in active obedience, He comes in and abides in [you]."[2] And it is to this degree that you will experience peace.

If you are now willing for your heart to be open to receive, ask God to open it wide. This is His work (Acts 16:14). Once again everything begins with God and ends with Him, for He is all in all: "In Him we live and move and have our being" (Acts 17:28). Your part is to join Him in the journey.

If God is all in all, what else can you receive besides His love, mercy, grace, and your gift of faith? Everything! All the marvelous blessings you have come from God. There is nothing good you possess that did not come without His assistance. All the good gifts you receive in the future will also come from Him. Open your hands and heart now and receive the wonderful blessings, mercy, grace, faith, and love God is pouring into your heart. Receive them through His Word by faith, for the Word of God contains His creative power.

God calls those things that are not as though they were for a reason. It is because He can make them come into reality. Jesus, as the Word, has creative power (John 1:1, 14); but it is also in the written Word, the Bible, that Christ came to fulfill. The Bible is described as "living and powerful, and sharper than any two-edged sword, piercing even to the division of soul and spirit, and of joints and marrow, and is a discerner of the thoughts and intents of the heart" (Heb. 4:12). It contains the life and path to freedom and peace that you desire. Feed on it. Receive it as a seed and allow it to put its roots deep down into the foundations of your heart. From here it will sprout and grow upward toward God as you keep receiving by faith. It is watered by the Spirit so that your faith can spread its leaves providing a canopy, a haven for others to shelter beneath. Open your heart and receive, relax and yield to these blessings.

GETTING REAL

Do I freely receive from friends when I am in need?

Am I open and willing to receive from God?

List some of the things God has given you.

Am I enjoying His gifts? If not, why not?

What do I still need to open my heart to receive?

Are there some things I am only partially receiving and God wants to give me more?

What are they?

Am I willing to dare to become like a little child in my whole self and open my hands to receive more of God's gifts in full?

Will I take the wrapping off my gifts?

What is inside?

Chapter Twelve

YIELDING

Now with God's help, I shall become myself.
—SOREN KIERKEGAARD[1]

ONCE YOU HAVE arrived at the place of believing, have made the first tentative moves toward receiving, have dared to unwrap the beautiful paper enclosing your gifts and are holding them in your hands—or should I say heart—the next step toward peace is to yield to what you have now believed and received.

What use is a new bicycle if you will not ride it? Or an umbrella if you never use it? When using these simple objects, you gain so much greater freedom—you can travel much faster on a bicycle than your feet. You can walk freely in the rain underneath an umbrella. Even a tree bends in a storm, yielding to the wind as it lashes its branches. In so doing it survives the storm. It is the trees that do not yield that snap and break.

By yielding you are submitting to what you know to be true. You know riding a bicycle is faster than walking and you know an umbrella can keep you drier from the rain. In the same way, by yielding to God's sovereignty, mercy, grace, and love using your faith, you are bending to His will. This enables His will to be done on earth in your life just as it is done in heaven instead of your will being done, which has landed you in this place of anxiety. By yielding to His will, you are submitting to the reality that God knows best, even if you cannot understand some of His decisions along the way. "Submit to God," the apostle James commands (James 4:7). As a result you will discover a treasure chest of benefits. By yielding to Him you are positioning yourself in the perfect place for receiving more.

Probably the greatest immediate blessing from yielding, and therefore submitting, to God, is that Satan is repelled and runs far away from you. The remainder of the verse quoted above reveals this order of events. "Submit to God. Resist the devil and he will flee from you." Submission to God must come first for the desired result of Satan's expulsion from your life to become a reality. It is Satan's temptations and your flesh that cause you to become anxious, so it is wise to get rid of at least one of your foes as quickly as possible. Resist Satan in Jesus' name, identifying with Christ in your heart, and he is compelled to disappear.

Yielding your flesh to God is your next problem, and often the greatest, but this can also lead to the greatest blessing—a deep intimacy with God. To yield your flesh to God means you are yielding your right to yourself. This is your independence, your claim to fame—and shame! Each part of your soul must be fully yielded in your submission to God's sovereignty; this includes your mind, will, and your emotions, and each of these has their unique way of resistance.

Perhaps you cling to intellectualism or negative thinking; perhaps you harbor a secret addiction or an unhealthy passion such as a desire for personal glory; or perhaps you express your emotions freely disregarding the consequences to others, causing them emotional damage and unnecessary pain. Regardless of your unique personal claims to independence, as you receive God's mercy, grace, and love, you will discover you are more and more able to yield these parts of your soul because your faith will grow as you choose to believe the truth about who God is and what He is like. As you begin to become one with Him, allowing His Spirit to change you from the inside, you will begin to exhibit His wonderful character attributes as you allow them to infiltrate your own flesh.

As you journey along this process, it is important to remember that yielding requires a response on your part. You need to respond to and apply God's Word in every area of your life. Just listening is not enough. Each part of your flesh must be brought into agreement with God's will and ways. Your mind needs to agree with God's thoughts, even though He says:

> *My thoughts are not your thoughts, Nor are your ways*
> *My ways.... For as the heavens are higher than the earth,*
> *So are My ways higher than your ways And My thoughts*
> *than your thoughts.*
> —ISAIAH 55:8–9

God has greater plans for you than you have ever imagined; and as you purposefully yield to His thoughts, accepting them as truth, your own thoughts will move closer toward His thoughts as He gives you fresh revelation, wisdom, and knowledge. The distance between the two will shrink until you and God become one. You will be in complete agreement. There will still be times when God will confound you because He is mysterious and endlessly resourceful. But your trust will grow to enable you to walk blindly at these times, in faith, not knowing where you are going yet still standing firmly on the foundation of your belief in who God is, feeling assured and peaceful within your "not knowing." This is how Abraham walked when he was called to leave his homeland not knowing where he was going. Author Betty Skinner reflects on this as recorded in a book about her life: "Acceptance of our 'not-knowing' brings forth a complete transformation of self if we will trust it. Its purpose is purification and purgation and leads ultimately to freedom—freedom to be who God created us to be, to love and live in God, and to be filled with God."[2]

Next, your will needs to yield to His will so that you actually want the plans God has established for you since before the world began. King David's reflection applies to you too:

> *Your eyes see my substance, being yet unformed. And in*
> *Your book they all were written, The days fashioned for*
> *me, When as yet there were none of them*
> —PSALM 139:16

You must yield your daily routine, your intentions, and your motivations to God, for He says, "By grace you have been saved through faith, and that not of yourselves; it is a gift of God, not of works, lest anyone should boast. For [you] are His workmanship, created in Christ Jesus for good works, which God prepared beforehand that [you] should walk in them" (Eph. 2:8–10). God knows the plans He has for you. Ask Him to reveal them so that your will and His may be joined in union. Seek Him in quietness and solitude so you may hear His voice clearly. Read His Word daily so He may give you wisdom, understanding, and discernment. And understand that "it is God who works in you both to will and to do for His good pleasure" (Phil. 2:13). Then follow through with what He says.

Lastly, your emotions must yield to God. As you explore His Word and begin to experience the character of Christ as He changes you from the inside out, you will begin to respond to circumstances as He does. All your varied emotions and personality will remain intact. Christ was not a depleted, vague, unemotional man. He displayed the same full range of emotional responses you possess, from joy and love to anger and hatred. However, when He reacted to circumstances and people, He did so without sin. He did not respond from selfish ambition or self-protection but always to give God glory. This was true even when His emotional response was extremely vigorous, such as the day He overturned tables and drove the moneychangers out of the Temple (Matt. 21:12). Or there was the time when He seemed to procrastinate, turning up so late to comfort his friend Lazarus that the man died. His late arrival gave opportunity to raise him from the dead bringing even greater glory to God. As you yield your emotions to Christ, you will begin to feel them gradually transform. You will begin to love as He loves, rejoice as He rejoices, and hate as He hates. Your damaged emotions from the past will be healed and restored (Ps. 147:3).

Through yielding, you will become more like the "you" God designed you to be. You will be enabled to fulfill His plan for your life in greater detail. Your yielding opens doors for greater revelation and intimacy. The blessings attached to this deepening relationship are indescribable. The disciple who yielded the most to Jesus was also the one who became closest to Him. John leaned on His Master's shoulder and from this intimate position he asked intimate questions. When Jesus told His disciples that someone would betray Him, "leaning back on Jesus' breast, [John] said to Him, 'Lord, who is it?'" (John 13:25). And he was given the answer. The other disciples sensed this intimacy between Jesus and John, and Peter later asked, "But Lord, what about this man?" As a result of Jesus' answer the saying went out among the brethren that John would not die, but this is not what Jesus said (John 21:21–23). Read this passage and notice that in John's yielding and intimacy and in Peter's watching, they were both blessed and both came to know Jesus as Lord in greater measure.

Yielding, for all the treasure it unleashes, is not the final step, however. In yielding you bend your mind, will, and emotions to God, much as a flower leans toward the sun, opening its face to receive the glow of life-giving light, lengthening its petals to display their beauty, allowing its core to bloom for a season. The rain may fall, yet the petals remain open, the sun may shine yet they remain extended, the flower lives to fulfill its purpose, whether growing in a window box to brighten an invalid's day or hidden from the sight of man in the far reaches of a desert where only God's eyes can enjoy its season. To achieve its full potential, however, yielding must be followed by full surrender.

GETTING REAL

Am I willing to yield my mind to God to begin to experience "the mind of Christ"?

If not, why not? If I am willing, how can I do this?

Am I willing to yield my will to God, to want what He wants?

If not, why not? If I am willing, how can I do this?

Am I willing to yield my emotions to God to be restored?

If not, why not? If I am willing, how can I do this?

As I dare to yield, do I believe I will survive the storms of life?

What comes after yielding?

Chapter Thirteen

SURRENDERING

We need faith that has overcome the world and sacrifices the visible to be free for the spiritual to take possession of it.
—ANDREW MURRAY[1]

YIELDING IS A little like reaching out your hand, holding your favorite toy to give to your friend—and then what? And here is the important question. For if you are merely going to snatch it back again or allow your friend to play with it for a little while then retrieve it, what are you doing? You are simply lending it. Your act of yielding can end here; but this is not the place of real blessing and deepening intimacy with God, although it is a start.

You need to be prepared to give your favorite toy away forever, to say goodbye to it for eternity, to surrender it. This is what God requires of you. He wants you to give Him your right to yourself, your right to your own unique ways of thinking, your own desires and dreams, and your own ways of feeling and behaving. This is so much more than simply yielding for a limited time. Once you have given something away, you never have a right to take it back again.

Are your insides cringing at this suggestion? You may be thinking: *Then I won't be able to* _____ (fill in the action). *Then I might not be able to see my friend* _____ (fill in the name). *Then I can't* _____ (fill in the emotional reaction) *when I get mad/sad/glad.* If this is your response, then you are looking at this question from the viewpoint of your unregenerate "flesh" and are not "walking in the Spirit" with God. Paul says, "Walk in the Spirit, and you shall not fulfill the lust of the flesh" (Gal. 5:16). Let's take a moment and discover what surrender looks like when you walk in the Spirit:

- It means you no longer have your right to yourself.

- It means you will obey God unconditionally no matter what He asks of you.

- It means you will have closer intimacy and friendship with Him.

- It means He will share the thoughts on His mind and His wisdom with you (the mind of Christ).

- It means He will guide you continually and always lead you to the best solutions to your problems.

- It means you are continually under His protection.

- It means He will always provide for you.

- It means He will lead you on mighty adventures.

- It means you can never be separated from His love.

- It means you will never have any reason to fear adversity or pain (even though you may experience them).

- It means you will be filled with His joy.

- It means you will be filled with His Spirit.

- It means you will be filled with His peace that surpasses human understanding regardless of your circumstances.

Surrendering doesn't sound so terrifying after all, does it? It is giving up what you never can control to Someone who can and who has your best interests at heart. And why would you do this? Besides being wise, sensible, and therefore logical, it is simply your love response to God's almighty love for you. Theologian and missionary Stanley Jones puts it this way:

Between two persons there is no love without an inward self-surrender to each other. If either one withholds the essential self from the other, love is blocked; it will not spring up no matter how hard you try to love around and past that core of an unsurrendered self. So between you and God there can be no love without an inward self-surrender. Not the surrender of this thing, or that thing, but the surrender of you, the essential you.[2]

True self-surrender, which naturally leads to humble obedience, is the evidence of your love for God. The disciple John reveals: "For this is the love of God, that we keep His commandments. And His commandments are not burdensome" (1 John 5:3). Remember, this is the disciple who had the most intimate relationship with Christ. He knew through experience. Perfect surrender equals perfect obedience, and this obedience, as we have seen, must come from the heart. As Oswald Chambers says:

All the blessings of God in salvation and sanctification, all the Holy Spirit illumination are ours not because we obey—they are ours because we have put ourselves into a right relationship with God receiving Jesus Christ the Lord, and we obey spontaneously. We are not blessed through mechanical obedience but by receiving from Jesus something that enabled us to obey without knowing it, and the life was flooded with the power of God.[3]

Perfect surrender cannot occur apart from faith. As Andrew Murray points out in his quote heading this chapter, you need to leave the world behind and the influences that so easily ensnare you; the opinions of friends and enemies, the pull of ungodly interests are not part of God's will for your life. Even the pull of the good instead of the best must be released so that you are free to enter fully into the freedom God has for you and the abundant life and peace He wishes to give you. Faith resists all that is not of God to allow you to yield and surrender to all that is of God.

Faith in who God is and what He has done for you gives you the grit to work through the issues. Hope gives you the motivation to persevere, and surrender prepares you for and ushers you into this new life of trust in God, free from the tyranny of anxiety.

Surrender goes much further than submission. You can outwardly submit to a tyrannical or authority figure for the sake of peace while inwardly biding your time waiting for the opportunity to rebel, whereas true surrender is from the heart. It encompasses abandonment. Christ is our ultimate example. He lived a life of perfect surrender to His Father. He said, "For I have come down from heaven, not to do My own will, but the will of Him who sent Me" (John 6:38). His Father affirmed this at Jesus' baptism when He spoke from heaven, saying, "You are My beloved Son; in whom I am well pleased" (Luke 3:22). Jesus further explained this union later in His ministry by saying, "The Son can do nothing of Himself, but what He sees the Father do; for whatever He does, the Son also does in like manner" (John 5:19). His surrender not only encompassed His obedient behavior but also included every word that came from His mouth, revealing His complete harmony with His Father's thoughts. He said, "I do nothing of Myself; but as My Father taught Me, I speak these things" (John 8:28). This perfect relationship the Father and Son experience, with the Son in perfect surrender to His Father's will, is the same quality of relationship you are called to develop with God.

Christ had to go through His agony of decision and choose to surrender the last vestige of His flesh in the Garden of Gethsemane to achieve this, just as you also need to surrender all of who you are to Christ so that you may enter into the fullness of life and peace available to you. Jesus says, "Whoever desires to come after Me, let him deny himself, and take up his cross, and follow Me" (Mark 8:34). Your cross is your decision to surrender and obey no matter what. The choice is yours. However, if you choose not to surrender this right to your own independence, Jesus also makes it clear what will happen. He says, "Whoever desires to save his life [on his terms] will lose it, but whoever loses his life for My sake and the gospel's will save it" (v. 35). If you choose not to surrender your life fully to Christ, even though you may gain much in worldly possessions and paraphernalia, you will lose your soul and any hope of true peace. The Message Bible states it quite plainly:

> *Anyone who intends to come with me has to let me lead. You're not in the driving seat; I am. Don't run from suffering; embrace it. Follow me and I'll show you how. Self-help is no help at all. Self-sacrifice is the way, my way, to saving yourself, your true self. What good would it do to get everything you want and lose you, the real you? What could you ever trade your soul for?*
> — MARK 8:34–37, THE MESSAGE

What a challenge! How do you muster the courage? Even Christ did not accomplish this in His own strength, for He said, "He who sent Me is with Me. The Father had not left Me alone, for I always do those things that please Him" (John 8:29). Just like Jesus, you cannot live this life of surrender in your own strength. You need to be empowered by the very power of God. It is only God's Spirit within that can give you the power to do your part and surrender your flesh. God works with you within you, just as He did with Jesus, as you surrender all of who you are to Him.

Are you willing to allow the Spirit of God to empower you, to enable you to live the abundant life of inner peace He died to give you? This is not a one-time decision. It is a way of life—continually yielding, continually surrendering, continually obeying, and continually receiving further power and revelation. Andrew Murray again explains:

> *If there is anything holding you back, or any sacrifice you are afraid of making, come to God and prove how gracious your God is. Never be afraid that he will command from you what he will not bestow. God comes and offers to work this absolute surrender in you.*[4]

This magnificent and courageous journey is a personal, intimate moment by moment walk with God your Father, just as Jesus walked. It is from this position you are free and able to enter His supernatural rest.

GETTING REAL

Which parts of me am I not surrendering to God?

Why am I holding back?

What am I afraid of?

Are my fears valid?

If I choose to surrender to God, what will my relationship with Him be like?

What was Jesus' relationship with His Father like?

Was Jesus anxious in His relationship with His Father? Explain.

Am I willing to totally surrender myself to God now?

Chapter Fourteen

REST

My soul finds rest in God alone; my salvation comes from him. He alone is my rock and my salvation; he is my fortress, I will never be shaken.
—PSALM 62:1–2, NIV

AS A RESULT of surrendering your whole self to God, you will find yourself transported into a remarkable open space of rest. It is a place where you will feel continually in God's presence. The flurry of the world and all action around you will still be there and you will still be able to respond to it appropriately, but it will no longer have the power to disrupt this new peaceful spiritual space you are walking in. You entered as a result of your total surrender to God and the consequent level of sanctification that results from this, and you will remain here as you continue surrendered and surrendering. Feeling one with God, you will feel settled on the inside, no longer torn by the ravages of life and other people's expectations and desires, no longer torn by your own double-mindedness and doubt. This is the place of real peace. We will further explore the dimensions of this peace in the next chapter but now let's briefly explore the contrast between deciding to turn away from this wonderful place and wandering through the entrance into this new plane of existence and freedom.

The Israelites were warned that if they refused to obey God they would never find rest no matter where they went in the world and instead, through their disobedience, would receive a "trembling heart, failing eyes, and anguish of soul" (Deut. 28:65). Anxiety is anguish of soul. It can give you a trembling heart!

God has no desire for you to live this way. Instead, He wants you to "rest in the LORD, and wait patiently for Him; Do not fret" (Ps. 37:7). The rest that God wants you to experience is a place of refreshment. He said, "'This is the rest with which You may cause the weary to rest,' And, 'This is the refreshing'" (Isa. 28:12). It is available as you remain in His presence walking "in the Spirit" in obedience to all He has shown you through His Word and by His Spirit. The Lord says, "Stand in the ways and see, And ask for the old paths, where the good way is, And walk in it; Then you will find rest for your souls" (Jer. 6:16).

Today this fulfillment is found only through abiding in Christ. Jesus said:

> Come to Me, all you who labor and are heavy laden, and I will give you rest. Take My yoke upon you and learn from Me, for I am gentle and lowly in heart, and you will find rest for your souls.
> —MATTHEW 11:28–29

Your soul is yearning for this rest. Reread the above verse and discover the secret of how to obtain it. There is only one way— walking with Jesus, yoked together learning His ways. And what a blessing to discover His ways are gentle and His expectations and goals are not beyond your capabilities each and every day. To realize He knows your weaknesses and failings and your deepest secrets, and yet even knowing all this, He still says, "Come to Me…take My yoke…learn from Me." Every person around you may want you to take *their* yoke. Institutions, charities, and even churches may want you to take *their* yoke also, but this is not God's plan. Jesus says you are only to take *His* yoke. This is enough!

You will fail to enter Christ's rest and remain in it if you harden your heart and fall into disobedience. This is what prevented the Israelites from entering God's rest (Heb. 3:7–11; 4:6). Instead, the only way through to your goal is to listen to God's voice for He is calling to you, today, right now. Are you listening?

What is He saying to you? What must you follow through with and do as a result?

Oswald Chambers warns:

> *Beware of anything that is going to split up your oneness with Him and make you see yourself separately. Nothing is as important as to keep right spiritually. The great solution is the simple one—"Come unto Me." The depth of your reality, intellectually, morally and spiritually, is tested by these words. In every degree in which [you] are not real, [you] will dispute rather than come....Jesus says, "Come unto Me and I will give you rest" i.e., Christ-consciousness will take the place of self-consciousness. Wherever Jesus comes He establishes rest, the rest of the perfection of activity that is never conscious of itself.* [1]

Your place of resting is a place of doing the work God has entrusted to you patiently.

You must "wait on the LORD" (Ps. 27:14). This waiting is an integral part of resting. Psalm 37:7 reveals, "Rest in the LORD, and wait patiently for Him." Oh, how difficult this can be at times! In Psalm 130 the writer reflects on this agony: "I wait for the LORD, my soul waits, And in His word I do hope. My soul waits for the LORD More than those who watch for the morning— Yes, more than those who watch for the morning" (vv. 5–6).Yet patience is an essential characteristic of those who wish to walk with God. It is not only a fruit of the Spirit often called "long-suffering" (Gal. 5:22), it is also a personal characteristic that God uses to stretch and extend you, to grow you into the person He wants you to become because it is a characteristic of God's own personality. He is called "the God of patience" (Rom. 15:5).

Even God waits, "Therefore the LORD will wait, that He may be gracious to you" (Isa. 30:18). He waits for your sake, to draw you into the place of restoration. "The Lord is not slack concerning His promise, as some count slackness, but is longsuffering toward [you], not willing that any should perish but that all should come to repentance" (2 Pet. 3:9). Is He waiting for you now? Waiting patiently for you to come to a place of reality, to confess sin still lurking within and join with Him in a oneness that will produce real life and peace, a place free from anxiety? Are you still harboring doubt, disbelief, or double-mindedness? Are you refusing to surrender the hold the world and your flesh still have on you? Are you refusing to dare to trust in the graciousness and love of your heavenly Father?

While waiting for you, God uses your waiting to build your patience. James reassures you, "Let patience have its perfect work, that you may be perfect and complete, lacking nothing" (James 1:4). This patience comes from the testing of your faith (James 1:3), which relates back once again to the trials you are facing today including your trial with anxiety. God is using your anxiety and the process you are going through right now to overcome it, to bring you out into the fulfilling life of rest He wants to give you where you are one with Him, walking in union in the power of His Spirit. You need to work with Him in this process, receiving His strength and wisdom, obeying all you know, yielding and surrendering to the truth and reality He is showing you. As your patience develops you will become stronger. There are no shortcuts. God wants you to experience genuine peace.

Maintaining the motivation to seek God's rest through patient endurance is empowered by your hope as you gain knowledge and experience of Christ.

> *[You] have access by faith into this grace in which [you] stand, and rejoice in hope of the glory of God. And not only that, but [you] also glory in tribulations, knowing that tribulation produces perseverance; and perseverance, character; and character, hope. Now hope does not disappoint, because the love of God has been poured out in [your] [heart] by the Holy Spirit who was given to [you].*
> —ROMANS 5:2–5

This hope, empowered by faith and God's love poured into your heart, does not grow faint because it sees the invisible: "[You] were saved in this hope, but hope that is seen is not hope; for why does one still hope for what he sees? But if [you] hope for what [you] do not see, [you] eagerly wait for it with perseverance" (Rom. 8:24–25). Hope of the unseen is firmly based on your knowledge of who God is, that all He says in His Word is true, and it allows you to enter into His kingdom today while you are still walking around on planet earth. This is your "walk in the Spirit."

Romans 5:2–5 (quoted above) reveals another truth about this wonderful place of rest you are entering. It is a place where you are joined in oneness with God, not through any effort on your part but through love: "Hope does not disappoint, because the love of God has been poured out into your heart by the Holy Spirit" (v. 5). It is God's love that will sustain you. It is God's love that gives you the hope you need to persevere. It is God's love that gave the Holy Spirit to pour this love into you. This is the place of perfect peace and patience. In his book *Christian Discipline*, volume 2, Oswald Chambers illustrates this amazing truth:

> *The patience of the saint may be illustrated by the figure of a bow and arrow in the hands of God. He sees the target and takes aim, He strains the bow, not to breaking-point, however severe the strain may seem to the saint, but to just the point whence the arrow will fly with surest, swiftest speed to the bull's-eye.*[2]

The bull's eye is your oneness with God where you are free from all anxiety and experience the rest and peace of God. This is your goal.

GETTING REAL

Have I entered into God's rest?

How do I get there?

What do I need to change to enter His rest?

Am I patiently enduring?

In which areas do I need to wait with greater patience?

Who or what is my hope in?

How is my hope sustained?

Chapter Fifteen

PEACE

*What you have learned and received and heard
and seen in me—practice these things, and
the God of peace will be with you.*
—Philippians 4:9, esv

As you live a life of obedience to God's ways aligned with His character savoring the truths you are taught from the Word and the Spirit, the God of peace will be with you living His life within you! Paul, having experienced this reality, uses himself as an example suggesting that as the Philippians watch and imitate him, they will be able to enter God's peace as a practical experience. Are you an example showing others the way to live in God's peace?

As you are probably now aware, the level of peace you display to others is in close proportion to the level of your closeness to God.

> *Reflected peace is the proof that you are right with God because you are at liberty to turn your mind to Him. If you are not right with God, you can never turn your mind anywhere but on yourself. If you allow anything to hide the face of Jesus Christ from you, you are either disturbed or you have a false security.[1]*

These words of Oswald Chambers may seem harsh, but they are real. The Bible says, "There is no peace...for the wicked" (Isa. 57:21). Andrew Murray confirms this, relating the relationship to one of abiding: "To the degree [your] heart is given to Him in faith and [your] will is given in active obedience, He comes in and abides in [you]."[2] It is this close abiding that leads to your experience of peace, even though circumstances around may seem out of control. And gradually as you learn to live in this new space, your fight with anxiety will become a distant memory.

Your response to your circumstances will reveal your level of abiding and, therefore, your peace. I have had many opportunities to prove this recently. Being diagnosed with breast cancer, receiving a partial mastectomy, going through radiation therapy, all while my son was getting married and my ex-husband was demanding the sale of our family home in the middle of my recovery all tested the reality of my peace. One night, after a particularly aggressive letter from my ex-husband's lawyer, I lay in bed, in pain, wondering if I would be able to sleep. I read God's Word and remembered the course of action I believe He had directed me toward. I prayed, surrendering everything into His hands, and then settled down. To my amazement I awoke fresh and bright at 7:00 a.m. It is very rare for me to sleep all night without waking once, so this was a miracle! My peace was proved real, tested in the fire of circumstances. And it has been many times since. Yours can be real too! And yours will also be tested!

You are directed to "seek peace and pursue it" (Ps. 34:14). As you read God's Word and allow its truth to melt into your heart, you are pursuing it. Psalm 119:165 says, "Great peace have those who love Your law, And nothing causes them to stumble." Jesus is your "Prince of Peace" (Isa. 9:6). Only as you seek and pursue Him will you find what you are looking for.

Peace is a result of the growth of your trust in God as you pursue Him, getting to know Him more. "You [God] will keep him in perfect peace, Whose mind is stayed on You, Because he trusts You" (Isa. 26:3). To maintain this peace your mind must be engaged in godly thoughts and pursuits. This does not mean ignoring uncomfortable facts. Instead it means taking these facts to God and asking for His perspective, then waiting patiently for His response. God is very practical. He knows you need the answers to real questions. Trust Him and He will lead you in His way, in His timing.

Before Jesus left this earth to join His Father in heaven He said, "Peace I leave with you, My peace I give to you; not as the world gives do I give to you. Let not your heart be troubled, neither let it be afraid" (John 14:27). His peace is a gift. Yet as with any gift, you need to receive it, unwrap it, and use it. And as we have discovered, this gift, like all the others, is only received and unwrapped as you join in oneness with Him. He says, "In Me you may have peace. In the world you will have tribulation; but be of good cheer, I have overcome the world" (John 16:33; see also Rom. 5:1, Eph. 2:14).

Peace is a fruit of the Holy Spirit dwelling within you (Gal. 5:22). As you receive Christ's gift, yielding to it and surrendering your own agenda, you will discover that the peace of God, His settled trusting relaxing peace, will rule in your heart (Col. 3:15). It will rule over the turmoil of the world, over the tyranny of time and circumstances; over problems in relationships; over doubt, disbelief, double-mindedness, despair, desperation, and depression. It will rule in your mind, in your spirit, in your heart; and it will allow you to rest in harmony under the shadow of the wings of your all-powerful Father resting in His sovereignty, in His perfect knowledge, and His perfect goodness. There is no better place to be.

It is time for you to take His wonderful gift of peace, receive it into your heart, and yield to its settling power—a power that is beyond your human understanding to comprehend. No one else will understand you either. They will marvel at your composure, your joy, and your trust no matter what your circumstances reveal; and so will you! Take this gift, receive it, unwrap it in awe. The Prince of Peace, Jesus Himself, is handing it to you personally right at this moment.

GETTING REAL

Am I experiencing God's peace?

If not, what is still stopping me from receiving it? Why am I allowing this to prevent me from receiving it?

Am I willing to be one with Christ, to abide in Him, and to allow His will to be fulfilled in my life?

Will I receive His gift of peace now?

Will I unwrap all that it holds?

Sit quietly with your gift. What is it like? How does it feel?

Describe your experience in your journal.

Chapter Sixteen

TOWARD FULFILLMENT

*Whatever your years, there is in every being's
heart the love of wonder, the undaunted challenge
of events, the unfailing childlike appetite for what
comes next, and the joy of the game of life. You are
as young as your hope, as old as your despair.*

—GENERAL DOUGLAS MACARTHUR [1]

IN YOUR JOURNEY through this book replacing the tyranny of anxiety with the wonderful powerful experience of God's peace that is so far beyond human understanding, you will have discovered that the journey requires a daring and eventual delight in gently resting and trusting in your Father's capable care. As you learn to live in this place more and more each day—for it is a daily walk, often a moment by moment walk—you will also discover that your peace is miraculously multiplied: "Grace and peace be multiplied to you in the knowledge of God and of Jesus our Lord" (2 Pet. 1:2).

It is through living in the knowledge of God and His Son Jesus and who they really are, that allows you to experience the supernatural reality of multiplying peace where freedom from anxiety and enjoyment in life is found. It is not available anywhere else. All other attempts to alleviate anxiety will only work temporarily at best; but as you seek and pursue peace in God, you will discover the results are far-reaching and permanent. In fact, the results are multiplied and multiplied again so that no matter what circumstances and fiery trials assault you, you will remain firmly established in His perfect peace. This surely is the miraculous supernatural gift of peace given by a supernatural God.

To ensure your journey continues, Larry Crabb reveals another truth which must also be embraced: "Finding God means to face all life both good and bad, with a spirit of trust...You know you are finding God when you believe that God is good no matter what happens."[2] Do you believe God is good no matter what happens in your life? No matter what trials assault you? Is God good through an experience of cancer? Is He still good through divorce and even death? The Bible says, "For the LORD is good; His mercy is everlasting, And His truth endures to all generations" (Ps. 100:5). It is because of His uprightness and goodness that He teaches sinners His ways and guides in the ways of justice (Ps. 25:8–10). God doesn't have to do any of this, but He wants to—because He is good and because He loves you. If it were not for His goodness, you would never have reached the point of salvation, for it is "the goodness of God [that] leads you to repentance" (Rom. 2:4). Jesus also reflects this powerful goodness. He was "God anointed...with the Holy Spirit and with power, who went about doing good and healing all who were oppressed by the devil, for God was with Him" (Acts 10:38).

Because God is good and all He does and is, is good, then it follows that everything He gives you and allows in your life can be turned to good no matter what the package looks like; even if it means facing terrible tragedy and deep pain for a season. It is within this profound potential for goodness, regardless of what the package looks like, that He wants to bless you. "Oh, how great is Your goodness, Which You have laid up for those who fear You, Which You have prepared for those who trust in You In the presence of the sons of men" (Ps. 31:19). His desire to give you good things includes everything you could ever need, from opportunity to practical necessities like health and strength and from peace to wholesome relationships. Nothing beneficial is excluded. James reassures you, "Every good gift and every perfect gift is from above, and comes down from the Father of lights, with whom there is no variation or shadow of turning" (James 1:17).

Yet let's be realistic. We do live in a sin-filled world with sin-filled imperfect people; there is no denying this. And sometimes sinful people seem to rule the hour. God's will is not always done; and we know God never sins, so He cannot cause someone to rape you, murder your brother, or commit adultery. Yet here is the mysterious wonder. Even within these evil constraints, in spite of other people's intentions and wickedness, God promises that everything He does for you is good. Even when others intentionally want to do you harm, God will bring benefit out of your circumstances for you, as you remain one with Him, trusting Him. He promises this: "And we know that all things work together for good to those who love God, to those who are the called according to His purpose" (Rom. 8:28).

Joseph found this to be true when he finally said to his brothers after they had treated him so badly, "As for you, you meant evil against me; *but God* meant it for good, in order to bring it about as it is this day, to save many people alive" (Gen. 50:20, emphasis added). Never forget the "*but God!*" Nothing is finished until God finishes it. Nothing is complete until God completes it. "For with God nothing will be impossible" (Luke 1:37).

As this understanding seeps through your mind and is joined by God's revelation of Himself and His holy character, and as you meditate on these truths, you can come to the place where you can say deep within your heart, "Yes, God is good through cancer, divorce, and death. Yes! God is always good!" Cancer, divorce, and death are never good within themselves. They may be caused by other people's sin, our own sin, the fallenness of the world, or the evil schemes of Satan; but God is never defeated by any of these things. He can still bring victory and peace into your world in spite of and through them. God can be found through the pain of cancer, the upheaval of divorce, and through the valley of the shadow of death. He is available wherever you may be right now if you seek Him with all your heart. He wants to bring victory, fulfillment, rest, and peace into your life. This victory and fulfillment and the accompanying peace they bring can only be found in His intimate presence.

As you seek God and come to know Him more, as you develop your relationship with Him so that you become one in Christ with Him, you will discover your anxiety vanishes like the mist in the morning sun. Where you stand in one with Him, there is no place for confusion or worry because you stand in the full power of God Himself. His power contains all of who He is, His glory, His wisdom, His grace, His holiness, His justice, His protection, His perfection, and His love. He dwells within you. As you walk with Him sharing His yoke, you are in His will, you are standing together, and nothing can prevail against you under His care.

If you become anxious again for a period of time, know this is a signal you are moving away from His holy presence traveling in the wrong direction. Be aware you will still feel the wide range of varied emotions from deep sadness or tremendous anger to elated happiness within His will. You do not become a robot. But your God is not a God of confusion (1 Cor. 14:33), He is the Prince of Peace. Change your direction and begin again to move closer to Him, becoming all you were created to be in all the fullness and freedom Christ died to give you. To stay whole, to stay fulfilled in every moment through every circumstance no matter how devastating they may seem, you must stay at one with Him. Here, and only here, is your peace.

GETTING REAL

Do I believe God is good?

Are there some circumstances I do not believe He can turn to good? What are they?

Is my assessment true? (What does the Bible say?)

Where is my fulfillment?

How can I know when I am moving away from God?

What can I then do?

Look back over your journey toward rest and peace, and rejoice in your progress.

Chapter Seventeen

FUTURE HOPE

Hope does not try to determine how God's way will be shown but remains open to new and astonishing manifestations of God's presence at work in the circumstances of life.
—BETTY SKINNER[1]

YOUR GOD HAS a magnificent plan for your life. He is good. He loves you and wants to have a meaningful, intimate relationship with you. He is a God of peace and not of confusion and He wants you to share in His peace. It is His gift to you. To reach this place of tremendous peace requires believing God is who He says He is. It requires being open to receive all the wonderful gifts, both spiritual and natural, that He bestows on you. It requires yielding to this relationship in a fresh and positive way, expecting good things from your good God. Ultimately, it requires surrender of your right to yourself as you dare to trust your sovereign King, your Lord, who has the wisdom, goodness, and ability to direct and guide you in life in the way that will bring the greatest blessing in the long term.

From this new position life becomes an amazing adventure, and as you embrace it you will wake each morning longing to see what He will do next. How will He manifest Himself today? How will He speak to you about your latest dilemma or answer your latest question? How will He reveal His wisdom? How will He comfort you through sorrow? How will He lead you into His victories? How will He share His love, pouring it into your heart? How will He teach you to love and share more deeply with others with His own love and wisdom?

Each day is a new parcel of life, a package to be unwrapped

and marveled at, to be lived to the full, to be shared with others. Each day you have the opportunity to move closer toward God instead of further away from Him. Which will you choose? Do you choose to flee from Satan and worldly lusts and "walk in the Spirit" instead of the flesh? Each day you can find something new to praise Him for. Each day you can search His Word and spend time talking to Him in prayer, getting to know Him more, expanding your knowledge as you grow in wisdom and share the mind of Christ. Each day you can listen more intently to the Word He is communicating through His written Word or through the whispering of His Spirit within your spirit. Each day you can seek His will and wisdom and revel in His love.

Every day will bring new avenues of joy, new thrills of laughter, new depths of peace and also of pain. The kingdom of God has come with this fullness of life. It is within you. Explore your freedom, revel in your safety, run into your Father's arms, join with Him in the dance of life. And when you are weary, sit quietly in the space He provides beside Himself, retreat under the shadow of His wings, drink from His everlasting waters of life, and be restored soaking in His eternal peace. It is His peace He gives to you. This is the peace and rest that demolishes all strongholds of anxiety.

As you join with Him in oneness of Spirit, there is no longer any space for doubt, double-mindedness, or unbelief. Instead there is a oneness, a yoke, a strong bond that cannot be broken that permeates your very soul and spirit to the deepest level. And from here deep within your core the fragile petals of trust will bloom.

The good soil has been laid, the water has softened the earth, the seed has finally germinated, and new life has begun. This life is firmly founded in a hope that will never disappoint. It is grounded upon the solid foundation of an everlasting God who is eternally good and wise. This life extends beyond the boundaries of the natural, for it is fed and nurtured from the spiritual. It is a supernatural life.

You will not always know what is to come. All the surprises

you receive will not always seem pleasant, but they will result in a complete transformation of yourself as you dare to trust in your God who is leading the way. These surprises, both good and painful, will lead you into experiencing a profoundly deep sense of freedom, belonging, and acceptance. You will be heralded into a new life of love and completeness, filled with God. This is your life free from anxiety. You may not always know what is to happen, you often may not understand, but you will know the One who does. To live in such a blessed place is the privilege God gives to all His children, and you are one of them. What are you waiting for? It is time to join Him in this relationship of deep, intimate love and trust so that your joy may be full and overflowing.

Epilogue

I SURVIVED MY operation, radiotherapy, and the pain and difficulty all this entailed; and my peace has not been broken, in fact it has grown. God is so faithful. There were complications. A nurse took out a tube too early and I had to return to have the wound drained three times. However, God remained faithful. I have now been cleared. My son is now happily married. I managed to deliver my speech at his wedding in spite of the swelling and pain. It was a wonderful day. I was told my speech was the funniest! I was grateful. My daughter who was in such pain for so long is now also happily married, and although she still has occasional headaches, is full of life. My brother is still unemployed. My father has just had his ninety-first birthday and is in great health. I stayed in my house until I fully recovered and had come to the place where I was ready for change. My new home is by the sea, and I walk on the beach in delight and gratitude every day. My first grandchild, four years after my son's wedding, has just had her first birthday. What joy this brings! And yet troubles continue. Unrelated to my previous breast cancer I have just been diagnosed with level four esophagus and liver cancer and must undergo chemotherapy in the hope of extending my life for one to two years, so they say. Yet I wonder! What does God say? He is the Author and Finisher of my life. It is He who numbers my days. He supplies all my needs. Our generous God invites us all to "taste and see that the LORD is good" (Ps. 34:8) regardless of our circumstances; and as we do we are heralded into His glorious peace. I can feel it still, it has not left me, a wondrous open space filled to overflowing with freedom and joy, far from the tyranny of anxiety.

Notes

CHAPTER ONE

1. J.I. Packer, *Knowing God* (London, UK: Hodder & Stroughton, 1984), 303.
2. Anne Laidlaw, *Know God More* (Lake Mary, FL: Creation House, 2009)—my book will help you develop a deeper scriptural understanding of who God really is if you wish to study further.

CHAPTER TWO

1. Elisabeth Elliot, *These Strange Ashes* (Grand Rapids: Revell, 2004), 127.
2. Oswald Chambers, *My Utmost for His Highest* (1935; repr., Grand Rapids: Discovery House, 1992), 280.

CHAPTER THREE

1. E. Stanley Jones, *Abundant Living* (London, UK: Hodder & Stroughton, 1946), 77.
2. Elisabeth Elliot, *On Asking God Why* (Grand Rapids: Revell, 2000), 100.

CHAPTER FOUR

1. 1. There are many online references. Mine is adapted from http://www.whitedovebooks.co.uk/nlp/anchoring.htm.

CHAPTER FIVE

1. G.K. Chesterton, *Orthodoxy* (New York: Image Books, 1959), 95.

CHAPTER SIX

1. John MacArthur, *Anxious for Nothing* (Colorado Springs: Victor, 2006), 44.
2. Ibid., 126.

CHAPTER SEVEN

1. Andrew Murray, *Daily Experience with God* (New Kensington, PA: Whitaker House, 1984), 48.
2. Ibid., 151.
3. Laidlaw, *Know God More*, 4.

CHAPTER EIGHT

1. A.W. Tozer, *The Pursuit of God* (Camp Hill, PA: Wingspread, 1948), http://worldinvisible.com/library/tozer/5f00.0888/5f00.0888.c.htm (accessed June 24, 2012).

CHAPTER NINE

1. Chambers, *My Utmost for His Highest*, 280.

CHAPTER TEN

1. Murray, *Daily Experience with God*, 66.
2. Smith Wigglesworth, *Greater Works* (New Kensington, PA: Whitaker House, 1999), 525.

CHAPTER ELEVEN

1. Henri J.M. Nouwen, *The Inner Voice of Love* (New York: Image Books, 1999), 49.
2. Murray, *Daily Experience with God*, 138.

CHAPTER TWELVE

1. Soren Kierkegaard, *The Prayers of Kierkegaard* (Chicago: University of Chicago Press, 1956), 147.
2. Kitty Crenshaw and Catherine Snapp, *The Hidden Life* (Colorado Springs: NavPress, 2006), 202.

CHAPTER THIRTEEN

1. Murray, *Daily Experience with God*, 148.
2. Jones, *Abundant Living*, 25.
3. Oswald Chambers, *God's Workmanship* (Grand Rapids: Discovery House, 1953), 23.
4. Andrew Murray, *The Believer's Absolute Surrender* (Minneapolis: Bethany, 1955), 78.

CHAPTER FOURTEEN

1. Chambers, *My Utmost for His Highest*, 232–233.
2. Oswald Chambers, *Christian Discipline*, vol. 2 (London, UK: Oswald Chambers Publications Association, 1938; Edinburgh, UK: Marshall Morgan & Scott, 1965), 155–156.

CHAPTER FIFTEEN

1. Chambers, *My Utmost for His Highest*, 239.
2. Murray, *Daily Experience with God*, 138.

CHAPTER SIXTEEN

1. Douglas MacArthur, "Text of MacArthur's Address at Los Angeles Banquet," *New York Times*, January 27, 1955, 8, http://tmh.floonet.net/articles/macarthurspeech.html (accessed June 24, 2012).
2. Larry Crabb, *Finding God* (Grand Rapids: Zondervan, 1993), 106.

CHAPTER SEVENTEEN

1. Cranshaw and Snapp, 165.

Bibliography

Allender, Dan. *Bold Love*. Colorado Springs: NavPress, 1992.

Chambers, Oswald. *Christian Discipline*, vol. 2. London, UK: Oswald Chambers Publications Association, 1938. Reprint, Edinburgh, UK: Marshall Morgan & Scott, 1965.

————. *God's Workmanship*. Grand Rapids: Discovery House, 1953.

————. *My Utmost for His Highest*. 1935. Reprint., Grand Rapids: Discovery House, 1992.

Chesterton, G.K. *Orthodoxy*. New York: Image Books, 1959.

The Christian Life Bible. Nashville: Thomas Nelson, 1985.

Crabb, Larry. *Finding God*. Grand Rapids: Zondervan, 1993.

Crenshaw, Kitty, and Catherine Snapp. *The Hidden Life*. Colorado Springs: NavPress, 2006.

Dawson, Joy. *Forever Ruined for the Ordinary*. Nashville: Thomas Nelson, 2001.

Elliot, Elisabeth. *On Asking God Why*. Grand Rapids: Revell, 2000.

————. *These Strange Ashes*. Grand Rapids: Revell, 2004.

Haggai, John Edmund. *How to Win Over Worry*. Eugene, OR: Harvest House, 2001.

Jones, E. Stanley. *Abundant Living*. London, UK: Hodder & Stroughton, 1946.

Kierkegaard, Soren. *The Prayers of Kierkegaard*. Chicago: University of Chicago Press, 1956.

MacArthur, John. *Anxious for Nothing*. Colorado Springs: Victor, 2006.

Murray, Andrew. *The Believer's Absolute Surrender*. Minneapolis: Bethany, 1955.

————. *Daily Experience with God*. New Kensington, PA: Whitaker House, 1984.

Nouwen, Henri J.M. *The Inner Voice of Love*. New York: Image Books, 1999.

Packer, J.I. *Knowing God*. London, UK: Hodder & Stroughton, 1984.

Tozer, A.W. *The Pursuit of God*. Camp Hill, PA: Wingspread, 1948. Also available online at http://worldinvisible.com/library/tozer/5f00.0888/5f00.0888.c.htm.

Wigglesworth, Smith. *Greater Works*. New Kensington, PA: Whitaker House, 1999.

About the Author

ANNE LAIDLAW IS a professional counselor and supervisor in Auckland, New Zealand. She has developed and teaches Pastoral Care Courses "Helping People—A Biblical View of Restoration and Basic Counseling Skills," Parts One and Two. She spends as much time as possible writing, enjoying her three children—two married—and her new granddaughter. She speaks at conferences and retreats emphasizing getting to know God more deeply, entering into freedom in Christ and fulfilling our God given potential. She is the author of *Know God More*, *Kick Addiction*, and a children and adult novel, *Danger Park and Beyond*, which explores issues of leadership, responsibility, and freedom. Anne also enjoys walking and painting. She is the granddaughter of Robert Laidlaw, author of *The Reason Why*, which has over fifty million copies in print.

To Contact the Author

www.annelaidlawministries.com

OTHER BOOKS BY ANNE LAIDLAW

No one plans to be an addict. It just sort of happens. One small decision after another adds up until you are bound in captivity with chains that were too weak to be felt until they are too strong to be broken. *Kick Addiction* lays out easy-to-understand steps towards freedom.

Available at www.amazon.com, good bookstores, and www.annelaidlawministries.com.

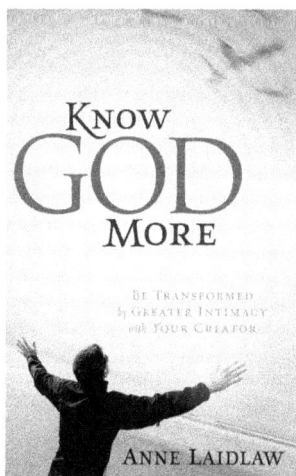

How can you trust someone you don't know? Build your faith! God's mysterious nature unravels as you seek Him.

Know God More explores forty-four characteristics of God that will build your faith and enhance your ability to embrace life to the full by empowering you to change positively. To the extent you *Know God More*, you will be able to fulfill the potential and live in the freedom He has for you.

Available at www.amazon.com, good bookstores, and www.annelaidlawministries.com.

*D*ANGER *PARK AND BEYOND*' (for 9–90 year olds) is an adventure story about rare and endangered animals in a wildlife park in New Zealand. Through extraordinary and terrifying circumstances, they escape into the wild and try to survive an unknown and misunderstood environment. In their new freedom and amidst a developing relationship between two young Black Lemurs, Rudo and Kemba, the animals face perils, betrayal, joy, and pain. This adventure explores the concepts of leadership, freedom and responsibility.

Available at http://www.amazon.co.uk/ Danger-Park-and-Beyond-ebook/dp/B006GVZI1S.

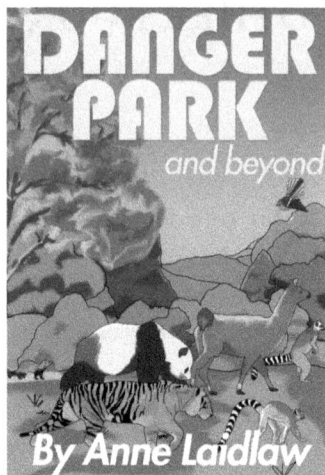